YOU, ME, AND THE VIOLENCE

21ST CENTURY ESSAYS
David Lazar and Patrick Madden, Series Editors

CATHERINE TAYLOR
YOU, ME, AND THE VIOLENCE

Mad Creek Books, an imprint of
The Ohio State University Press
Columbus

Library of Congress Cataloging-in-Publication Data
Names: Taylor, Catherine, 1964– author.
Title: You, me, and the violence / Catherine Taylor.
Other titles: 21st century essays.
Description: Columbus : Mad Creek Books, an imprint of The Ohio State
    University Press, [2017] | Series: 21st century essays
Identifiers: LCCN 2017019235 | ISBN 9780814254325 (pbk. ; alk. paper) |
    ISBN 0814254322 (pbk. ; alk. paper)
Subjects: LCSH: Drone aircraft. | Puppets. | Soldiers.
Classification: LCC PS3620.A93583 Y68 2017 | DDC 814/.6—dc23
LC record available at https://lccn.loc.gov/2017019235

Cover design by Jeff Clark
Text design by click! Publishing Services
Type set in Adobe Garamond, ITC Officina Sans, and M+ 1m

♾ The paper used in this publication meets the minimum requirements of the
American National Standard for Information Sciences—Permanence of Paper
for Printed Library Materials. ANSI Z39.48-1992.

9 8 7 6 5 4 3 2 1

In a scene from Truffaut's *The 400 Blows,* in a darkened room, we see the faces of children at a puppet show. They appear, at first, transfixed. Still. Lifeless. Then their mouths drop open wide as if unhinged. They bounce up and down jerkily in their excitement. Suddenly, their bodies all lean forward in one motion as if pulled by the same string. One child's hands fly abruptly to his face in horror. He twists as if moved by a rod from above. Another stiffly, but gently, tips his head to rest on the shoulder of his friend. Their eyes stare in one direction. They don't see us. They don't see Truffaut's camera. They don't see the puppeteers. They see only the wolf gnashing his jaw. Red Riding Hood screaming in his grasp. We watch them manipulated by the puppets and by Truffaut. We watch them not in the fullness of who they are, their histories, their changes, their relations. We see them only as they become puppets, become objects, and thus, paradoxically, become themselves.

I was longing for something other than bureaucracies of death, something other than the crisis under my fingertips every day. The usual murder. The general dampening. Spending time with puppets seemed like a good idea. Brainless, strange, potentially political, and tapped into the rapture part of my children's childhood (slipping fast away). Tapped into our little house on the edge of Appalachia, where my twelve-year-old lived in the basement, with its concrete floor and tiny window up high near the edge of the earth. Look at him, turning a large, cardboard refrigerator box into a Dada puppet-theatre. He has painted it red with the slogan "Dada Seigt!" scrawled on the back. He's added black curtains to the small head-height opening and straps that allow him to carry the contraption on his back as he rides around our small town on his bicycle. He has cut up poems that he reads in the voices of his puppets. One is a crab claw. One is a tiny replica of my boyfriend dressed as a gangster. Clay head, black cloth suit, white satin tie. Sometimes, a friend played her cello with him. One year, he went as Hugo Ball for Halloween. One year, he made me a miniature replica of a factory complete with a tiny puppet fist whose lever let it smash the paper smokestacks. His sense of possibility worked like a charm.

Think of puppets. Shadow, marionette, rod, sock, finger, avatar, persona. Think of big-nosed Punch and Judy whacking and pummeling each other on their little stage. Think of the swaying papier-mâché giants of political street theater, the disturbing meat puppets of Jan Svankmajer, the creepy doll heads of the Brothers Quay, the marionettes in *Being John Malkovich,* Basil Twist's string man, James Cameron's imperialist avatars, the sad inhabitants of the uncanny valley. There are pregnant puppets full of others, puppets made of ice that melt, and puppets of paper that burn. Think of Indonesian Wayang Kulit with its oil lamps and amber screens. Gamelan gongs hammered and clanging, rising and chiming. The black silhouettes of lacy, angular gods looming as they enter their epic battle. Figures sharpen and blur. Think of bug-eyed Ernie in his stripy shirt saying, "Gee, Burt" and snickering behind his hand. Puppets are only puppets when they seem to have no masters. When they seem to act on their own. Autonomous. Alive. Once we glimpse the master, the puppet becomes merely an object. A doll. Puppets are only puppets, are only truly themselves, when they seem not to be themselves, when we forget that they are puppets. This is the paradox of puppets, and our pleasure in them lies within this paradox.

The lure of puppets is a vitalizing enchantment. Puppets entice with their uncanny gestures, subtle and abrupt. A glide and then a lurch. Strange eyes. Shifting shadows. Black-clad operators in hoods and veils. Moving objects and only an occasional glimpse of the strings that lift them. We are enthralled by their power even as we know it is not truly theirs. Like a puppet, the drone is both an extension of the operator and an object unto itself. Something manipulated. A body with a distant mind. A form of visual ventriloquism. Like a puppet, the drone enthralls us with a power that is not its own. Drones have the strange appearance of autonomy found in robots, automata, and puppets. Unlike a puppet, a drone is not expressive. It likes to hide. It leans more instrumental than performative. Or does it? The bulging head, the high-pitched whine, even the nasty nicknames (Predator, Reaper, Vulture, Demon) slick back into the spectacle (that "autonomous movement of the non-living," as Guy Debord writes).[1] Drone potential, even if invisible, is part of the theatre of fear in the theatre of war. As is their tenacious vision. Their grainy trailers. Snuff film surveillance videos or "drone porn." The blurry insurgents, black or white, in heat sensor mode. Running. Stopping. Running. The crosshairs flashing. Sparkle on. You are cleared to engage. A pixelated black cloud. Then the deadly ending we came for; the figures now prone. Here, the drone as puppet slips behind the curtain and instead produces the stage itself, the proscenium screen framing the view from the pilot's Naugahyde Barcalounger or from our own comfy chair.

The drone hovers. Invisible and menacing. If you get a glimpse (which you won't), you might see the swiveling eye. Maybe it's looking at you. Maybe you're looking at it. Or through it. It depends who you are. My brother is an Air Force pilot. Not long ago, he called to say that he was being transferred to begin flying drones. Actually, I don't think he used the word *drone*, as he says this is a media slur freighted with fear. He uses the term *RPA,* or Remotely Piloted Aircraft. I think he prefers this to the military's other commonly used acronyms—UAVs, Unmanned Aerial Vehicles, or UAS, Unmanned Aerial Systems—as it keeps the pilot in the picture. Also, looking back, I'm not sure if he said he would be "flying" them. He may have said "operating," because, of course, you can't slip the bonds of Earth from behind the drone pilot's video joystick. My brother would no longer feel the plane vibrate within his body. He would no longer look out and catalogue the clouds. Billow, banner, arch, or anvil. Nimbus, cirrus, veil, or wall. He would no longer be moving through the air as birds do. But his plane would.

Broken Radio Comms   maneuvering on all four sides   *garbled radio*
copies you broken from Jaguar   understand   you're   experiencing
movement all around last known location   no   movement   here
at this time We are now tracking three vehicles and standby   Copy

Broken Radio Comms   Slasher03   Jag25   yeah
those vehicles are bad we're gonna have to get to work on trying to get enough to
engage from what we are hearing on ICOM traffic a QRF is coming in for a

                   Broken Radio Chatter   Roger   that   again   3
vehicles all seem to be predominately moving west bound off in the green space
we have our eyes on *Broken Radio Comms*   appears to be *unlawful*
personnel in   the back   Gonna take

missile power off   Copy   Just let it cool down

Slasher 03   JAG25   Jaguar go for Slasher   * Radio Static *
Slasher 03   JAG25   * Radio Static *   JAG25

Roger thinking about the situation   I'm pretty sure we are covered

Demonstration of hostile intent tactical maneuvering in conjunction with the ICOM chatter it would appear that they are maneuvering on our location and setting themselves up for an attack   Copy that

Broken Radio Chatter   up to 3 additional pax   Again that compound with the rendezvous there's an additional pickup truck appears hot and we're tracking multiple personnel throughout Slasher03

Roger   Is that a dude outside?

Slasher we can put down the sparkle   Going to fused   I see them right there

                    We are eyes on the west side of the river we are in fused if you
want to go ahead and throw down your sparkle   OK

                              I see a vehicle with flashing lights on

Sparkle on
                    Sparkle on

                              Call contact

                                    contact

                                          sparkle

In the darkened bedroom, a shadowy bird flies by. It disappears into the black. Someone adjusts the flashlight, and a dark rabbit twitches its nose; a knot of knuckles. In the pitch-black theatre, a green light scissors the void. Suddenly, an enormous head appears. The space vibrates with high-pitched screams. The static staring eyes tell us they're not real, but fail to reassure. We are in Bil Baird's Marionette Theatre on Barrow Street in Greenwich Village in the late 1960s. My memory does not include my mother, or even myself—only the black space that both numbs and attunes, the sound of Toto's chaotic barking, and the animistic intensity of willing him to step back. Step back.

Puppets let us see the processes of animation and displacement even as they make us forget them. It is a banal magic. See us transfixed. See how the puppet in turn puppets us. A puppet is an object that might move us with its movements. This is the fascination of anything remotely operated, an object that cannot move on its own, but does.

My brother first learned to fly when he was a neurobiology student working with homing pigeons. As part of his summer lab job, he would pack the birds into big, slatted, wooden crates, load them into his battered pickup truck, and drive them out into the country where he would release them and measure things like the odor gradient of the pines, the azimuth of the sun, the magnetic fields. Then, he'd drive back to the pigeon coop, or loft, where he'd lie out on the roof and sleep in the sun and dream whatever 19-year-olds dream, until the birds returned and woke him by ringing a bell rigged to their trap door. One day, after watching them fly off into the mystery of their instinct, he drove to the local airport and signed up for a flying lesson. Maybe it was the Swedish flight instructor named Elsa, or maybe it was what he called the "sports-car feel of a small plane," or maybe it was the sense he had that once in the air, as he said, "you really could leave everything behind." Antoine de Saint-Exupery said, "I fly because it releases my mind from the tyranny of petty things." At any rate, by the time he landed, at the end of his first lesson, he knew he wouldn't be going to vet school. He would be a pilot. All he wanted was to fly. That freedom. That autonomy.

Autonomy from routine. Autonomy from work. Autonomy from desire. Autonomy from responsibility. Autonomy from ruling tyrants. Autonomy most free when oblivious to autonomy. Autonomy most impossible when passive. Autonomy most exciting when attempted.

Flying for the military isn't really a place to find, or express, one's autonomy. It's mostly about following orders. But pilots do still make critical decisions, just as they always have, even if the majority of new Air Force pilots today will fly their planes from inside an office. The U.S. Air Force is currently training more drone pilots than all conventional fighter and bomber pilots combined.[2] The military advantages of this shift are significant, not the least of which is that it is safer for soldiers. And I have to confess that when my brother told me he was being transferred to fly drones, my first response was a sigh of relief. He would be safe. He wasn't going back to Iraq, or Afghanistan, or Yugoslavia, or Somalia, or any other place where people were trying to kill him, my little brother, the boy I grew up with, playing kick-the-can in the backyard and ping-pong in the basement, sitting next to each other in the backseat of the car for hundreds of sticky, dull, yet intimate, hours. After years of anxious adrenaline surges every time he was posted somewhere dangerous, I was glad to hear he would be out of harm's way. This is the way the idea of family, and of love, puppets us—the strings that attach me to my brother yanking me away from thinking further about the murky questions of the ethics of domination.

Plato wrote,

> We may imagine that each of us living creatures is a puppet made by gods, possibly as a plaything, or possibly with some more serious purpose. That, indeed, is more than we can tell, but one thing is certain. These interior states are, so to say, the cords, or strings, by which we are worked; they are opposed to one another, and pull us with opposite tensions in the direction of opposite actions, and therein lies the division of virtue from vice. In fact, so says our argument, a man must always yield to one of these tensions without resistance, but pull against all the other strings—must yield, that is, to that golden and hallowed drawing of judgment which goes by the name of the public law of the city . . . So a man must always co-operate with the noble drawing of law . . . In this wise, our moral fable of the human puppets will find its fulfillment.[3]

Inevitably, my flood of relief for my brother was shot through with doubt about the morality of drone warfare—this latest amplification of asymmetry in combat strength. The pilots so secure, the enemy so exposed, it is hard not to see the analogy to rifles versus arrows. It is hard not to feel that drones make for an unfair fight. Although, one might ask, when was war ever fair? And really, what would I prefer, bayonets? No. No, I wouldn't. Unless I can adopt a position of committed pacifism, maybe the more appropriate questions are the ones of "just war theory." When is war justified, and what is acceptable in war? Is it used only as a last resort? Is it proportional? Will it avoid creating an evil worse than the one it destroys? These are old questions, and I wonder if drones demand new ones. I ask my brother what makes drones different, and he writes, "The only difference is the pilot isn't in the plane."

At first, I object and point out that it is more complicated. The stealth issue, for instance. But, while the fact that drones are invisible matters, this isn't exactly new to warfare. Militaries have used camouflage and covert operations since before the Trojan horse. My brother asks, "Why are people so upset by a technology where the pilot is out of danger? We've had surveillance and reconnaissance platforms for a long time." And it is true that the Air Force had drones in Vietnam and similar technology even earlier. I answer that I think it has to do with the way drones were billed as being more accurate than conventional weapons but ultimately cause so many civilian deaths. My brother raises his eyebrows, and I know he's going to remind me that they haven't caused more civilian deaths than conventional warfare. I say, "The wedding parties." He says, "It has happened with other weapons. Apart from drones. Again, that doesn't have to do with drones. There've been plenty of civilian casualties with fighters and bombers. We've had that from . . . always. There were plenty of bombs dropped that killed civilian people, so it flabbergasts me that people think it is because of UAV technology. Don't they know we've always done that?"

So, maybe the only way "collateral damage" makes drones different from manned bombers is in the way drones expose, and thwart, expectations. That is, their potential accuracy was part of the rhetoric for their adoption, and their actual carnage caused disappointment, upset, and outrage, even though conventional bombing had been causing exactly the same kind of damage for years. Somehow, this felt different, even if it wasn't. In this way, maybe one of the most significant things about drones isn't how they *hide,* but how they *reveal* our distaste for killing, or at least the killing of innocents. In this way, we might see drones as an ironically effective tool for peacemaking if they can disclose that what their opponents oppose is not drones per se but unjust war. "Yes," my brothers says, "but are we talking about the impact of drones on war or about American politics? If you don't agree that we should be attacking terrorists where they are, that is a different issue and one you could argue, but that is not really about drones. The types of things we are using to go after them is immaterial. I don't deny that UAS are a little different, but in the end it is a platform that we created that delivers weapons. We're going to use all the technology at our disposal once we have decided to go after them."

True, the drone is a platform. It is a thing. And it isn't always deadly. Maybe you've felt the thrill as it carries a camera right into the incandescent heart of an explosion of fireworks, sparkling anemones of tinted light spilling bright clouds of gunpowder into your lap. Or maybe you've seen its tender view of a pod of dolphins bursting out of a curved blue sea while a mother whale and her baby loll together nearby, dear and luminous, just beneath the surface. Or, sometimes the drone plays the puppet. The other night, I saw John Cale perform with a group of dog-sized drones dressed in feathered headdress; they rose up awkwardly from their operators in the orchestra pit and flew back and forth over the audience blowing wind on us with their rotors. Like puppets, those anthropomorphized drones were alternately goofy and menacing, entertaining and embarrassing. So, yes, drones are just a platform.

But not everyone agrees that the nature of the technology is completely irrelevant. As Alex Rivera writes, "Saying 'technology doesn't carry out extra-judicial assassinations, tactics do' is as rigorous as saying 'guns don't kill people, people do' and he reminds us that, 'the drone assassin reduces the cost barrier to the tactic.'[4] Rivera is right, but it is hard to imagine a world where militaries agree not to reduce their cost barriers wherever and whenever they can. I try to imagine it anyway. The barrier to this utopian thinking is the accepted knowledge that there will always be new military technologies and the only possible point of intervention is at the level of control. Behind the drone, the pilot; behind the pilot, the military; behind the military, the president and his advisors. Who pulls their strings? The weapons and surveillance industry? The profit motive? Can "the people" manipulate this, or does the puppet analogy stop working here? The Nuclear Nonproliferation Treaty seems like one encouraging precedent, but only if other nations' drones start to similarly threaten the homelands of the superpowers.

When the feeling of a doomed inevitability rises, I force myself to rally by thinking about Martin Luther King Jr. saying,

> We as a nation must undergo a radical revolution of values. We must rapidly begin the shift from a "thing-oriented" society to a "person-oriented" society. When machines and computers, profit motives and property rights are considered more important than people, the giant triplets of racism, materialism, and militarism are incapable of being conquered. . . . Our only hope today lies in our ability to recapture the revolutionary spirit and go out into a sometimes hostile world declaring eternal hostility to poverty, racism, and militarism.[5]

Onstage, Dorothy emerges from behind a curtain, glides past the wizard's staring eyes, and deftly draws back another curtain, only to reveal another puppet. A recursive plunge. A childhood moment of ecstasy and terror.

A puppet speaks. A puppet is mute. A puppet is suggestive. A puppet is spooky. A puppet is pathetic. A puppet is helpless. A puppet is disturbingly real or unreal. A puppet is part of a performance. A puppet is magical. A puppet is a surrogate. A puppet is a proxy. A puppet is a disembodied self.

You can substitute a text for a puppet.
You can substitute a bomb for a text.
You can substitute a swarm for a self.

Waiting for a train, my son and I kill time in the station's tiny arcade. We are soldiers saving Earth from terrorists. We are good at it. The joystick is familiar and exciting. We control our avatars with ease and agility. These soldiers are our surrogates. Soldiers are our surrogates.

Broken unreadable say again   CLASSIFIED   Possible mortars
Good copy on that be advised personnel in the open by the vehicles moving
tactically definitely carrying objects   At this time
we cannot PID [Positively Identify] what they are however we've got eyes on and we
are working our best   Agree with all that we've already
determined that we've   uhh   How's your imagery looking

Was he talk'n to us   He was talking to Jag

                              Just keep looking maybe we'll see something
Roger ground force commander's intent is to destroy the vehicles and the personnel
right now showing that the individuals egressed the trucks holding cylindrical objects
in their hands   *radio static*

Go back to that guy down here   See if you can zoom in on that guy
'cause he's kind of like   What did he just leave there
Is that a *expletive* rifle?   Maybe just a warm
spot from where he was sitting can't really tell right now but it does look like an
object   I was hoping we could make a rifle out never mind
The only way I've ever been able to see a rifle is if they move them around when
they're holding them with muzzle flashes out or slinging them across their shoulders

radio static   Slasher, get eyes there

              broken radio chatter

He called for us but didn't answer back, probably can't hear us
Just stay on that truck if nothing else I'm gonna try and get you closer man   Copy

There we go   That's a little better huh?

They are all just hunkered down there waiting   Except for mister sitting duck
standing up there

Good copy on that no PID on weapons at this time only tactical movements
on the west side can you pass coords for the east please?

Sparkle down

Sparkle coming on

Sparkle on

Can you zoom in a little bit man let 'em take a look   At least 4 in the back
of the pickup   What about the guy under the north arrow does it look like
he is hold'n something across his chest   Yeah it's kind of weird how they all
have a cold spot on their chest   It's what they've been doing here lately
they wrap their *expletive* up in their man dresses so you can't PID it
                    Yeah just like that one there was a shot a couple of weeks ago
they were on those guys for hours and never saw them like sling a rifle but pictures
we   got   of   them   blown   up   on   the   ground   had   all   sorts   of

expletive

What's that guy got, the pickup lookout?   Yeah, I think he does have something
I think so   Jag25 Slasher03 Kirk97 it looks like the dismounted pax on the
hilux pickup on the east side is carrying something, but we cannot PID what it is at
this time but he is carrying something   He slung it on his
shoulder whatever it was, just switched arms with it or something, and is getting in
the truck

Alright so if the C-130 bugs out and we get a chance, dude you're pretty experienced
do what you think is right, stay with whoever you think has the best opportunity to
find something on them or follow the biggest group or

                                             do whatever you want to do

The screener is reviewing they think something is up with that dude as well I'll take a
quick look at the SUV guys   sorry   What do these dudes got

Yeah   I think that dude had a rifle   I do too   Slasher03   Jag25   Slasher03
Jag25   Jaguar25 go for Slasher   Roger   Given the distance and the
lack of weapons PID† we are having a hard time   (garble garble)
and also the same with fires   (garble)   to bring them in so we can
engage but we really need that PID to   (garble garble garble)   start
dropping   Yeah

they called a possible weapon on the MAM‡ mounted in the back of the truck.

All players all players from Kirk97 from our DGS the MAM that just mounted the
back of the hilux had a possible weapon read back possible rifle   Again
the other two on the east side of the river are also static with all folks loading

Kirk we notice that but you know how it is with ROEs§ so we have to be careful with
those ROEs   *broken radio chatter*   Sounds like they
need more than possible   Yeah

Believe we got most of that message but energy bled on a lot of it   Again
we appreciate working with you guys and have a safe, have a safe day

Copy Slasher03

That truck would make a beautiful target

---

† Positive Identification
‡ Military Age Male
§ Rules of Engagement

What are we to make of the frequently voiced concern that drone pilots kill more willingly and indiscriminately because of the video-game-like quality of their experience? If it is true, it is troubling. But I'm not convinced it is true. The media is full of reports that these soldiers, who have traded the intensity of the battlefield for a day of online tracking and killing at the office, have some of the highest stress rates in the armed services[6]—a fact that would suggest that they are not desensitized by distance in the way we might imagine. When I ask my brother why he thinks the PTSD rates are so high, he says, "There's no more band-of-brothers. You do the same job you used to do but without the same support." People also often comment on the disorienting phenomenon of soldiers who log off from a deadly operation only to drive to their kids' soccer games an hour away. In fact, recent studies suggest that some of the operators' stress might come simply from the long, monotonous hours of work, but the worst cases, those leading to PTSD, seem to occur primarily among operators who have seen, via video, casualties of women, children, or other civilians.[7]

Given the many reports of civilian drone casualties, as well as drone casualties classified as "militants" but who are killed in noncombat zones like Pakistan, is it possible that the evidence that soldiers suffer when they witness the suffering, and killing, of others might actually deter excessive use of drone force? Or will we just help them put on blinders? The military is already working on how to modulate exactly what drone operators will witness. On the pages of publications like *Science and Engineering Ethics,* military ethicists debate just how sharp the video images relayed by drones should be. Sharp enough to be accurate, but not so sharp that operators can't handle the reality of their actions.[8]

Ultimately, however, the solution looks like it might not be one of res-olution (of pixel counts), but of dissolution. Or, more accurately, the military solution to the problem of conscience will involve a literal dehumanization of military pilots as, increasingly, they will be taken out of the loop. This is what the military calls RMA, the Revolution in

Military Affairs, the rise of robotic, weaponized surveillance devices that are fully autonomous.

Things puppets can do to us: charm, deceive, captivate, fool, trick, remind, amuse, distract, bore, repulse, annoy, puzzle, transport, provoke, fascinate, stand in for, kill.

For now, most "autonomous mechanized combatant" vehicles and "tactical autonomous combatants" are still remotely controlled by human operators who are responsible for their actions. But soon, the puppets will be turned over to a new master, a computer code, an algorithm that will separate targets from non-targets for automated killing. Military ethics specialist Robert Sparrow asks us to consider whether the "development of robot weapons [will] generate an 'arms race to autonomy' thus effectively forcing the deployment of weapon systems in 'fully autonomous mode.'" In Iraq, we used not swords, but SWORDS, Special Weapons Observation Reconnaissance Detection Systems that are remotely controlled robots armed with machine guns. Some say we can expect swarms of nanodrones to be blown into cities in order to continuously datamine or monitor inhabitants, streaming information to automated weapon systems. "From this point on," Defense Watch reports, "nobody in the city moves without the full and complete knowledge of the mobile tactical center."[9]

Take at look at DARPA's hummingbird drone on YouTube, or the synchronized swarms of tiny nano-quadrotor robots that fly through a window in tight formation, hover, then spread out to cover the room to attack. Or consider the Hybrid Insect Micro-Electro-Mechanical Systems project where scientists have developed a moth-machine cyborg. The pupa is injected with electronic components and, after metamorphosis, the insect unfurls its wings and is flown by its human operator to a distant window where it flutters with the other bugs. Watching, recording, relaying the end of privacy.[10] The plan is to have them "weaponized." Nano- and genetic technology fuse in the latest forms of biological warfare. As Stephen Graham writes in his book *Cities Under Siege: The New Military Urbanism,* we can expect swarms of flying micro-robots that will target an individual's DNA by means of biological or genetic armaments injected into the subject's bloodstream. Graham quotes U.S. Air Force Colonel Daryl Hauck, who writes that, "Single microteeth-like devices could fit well within a blood vessel to carry and insert genetic material into cells."[11] Already, many of our war robots are designed for use in a system that, as Graham writes,

> Involves rapidly linking sensors to automated weapons so that targets that are automatically sensed and "recognized" by databases can be quickly, continually, and automatically destroyed. In US military parlance such doctrine is widely termed "compressing the kill chain."[12]

"Compressing the kill chain." Chilling, but what language of war isn't? And do I really imagine an end to war? No, I don't. So, why my continued hesitations, my anxieties about this technology? Perhaps they can be traced to the sci-fi fear that we will cede control to mindless robots, that we will surrender to them our autonomy. And even some within or close to the military share this concern. Edward Barrett, Director of Strategy and Research at the U.S. Naval Academy's Stockdale Center for Ethical Leadership, says, "The issue of autonomous lethal systems" or "the idea that you can use software that recognizes the targets and then makes a decision that's ethical to destroy targets, with no human intervention" is "ethically challenging."[13] He asks,

> Exactly what would these autonomous systems sense, decide, and do? Would they adequately distinguish combatants from non-legitimate targets such as bystanding civilians and surrendering soldiers—a task complicated by counter-countermeasure requirements? Would they adequately—i.e., at least as well as humans—comply with necessity and proportionality imperatives? Minimizing these possible in bello errors would require the elusive ability to credibly attribute bad results to a culprit—designers, producers, acquisition personnel, commanders, users, and perhaps even robots themselves. And if the notion of "robot

responsibility" ever becomes meaningful, would a self-conscious and willful machine choose its own ends, and even be considered a person with rights?[14]

If, as Barrett suggests, we enter an age when a robot can be "considered a person with rights," would this mean that instead of the drones being our puppets, we might become theirs?

Watch the puppet who looks up at the puppeteer. Watch the puppet master who disappears into the puppet. Watch the master bunraku operator when he is elevated to the highest status, when he is finally allowed to perform without the black hood that kept him hidden and thus becomes "dezukai," or "visible," a move that, implausibly, makes him even more a part of the puppet, who then seems doubly real. Watch Punch when he lurches to the edge of his little stage, looks down behind him and, to the delight of the crowd, yells out: "Move my hand. Move your hand. Inside me. Move me. Ah. Never mind. I'll do it myself."

It is a thrilling vision, but it is an illusion that the puppet is real. Just as it is an illusion that robotic weapons and deadly algorithms are autonomous. Because, in fact, a disembodied algorithm can't commit a war crime, but the one who chooses to deploy it, can. The real potential problem is not autonomous robots run amok, but an autonomous state run amok. I go to a parade on the 4th of July. Shriners in fezzes and miniature cars stream by, then fire engines, chrome choppers decorated with tiny American flags, cancer survivors, day care workers, children, and troupes of politicians and their aides. Finally, a group of performers moves steadily down the street. They are surrounded by a sky-blue banner that proclaims, "We're all in the same boat." Lagging several paces behind them, a papier mâché Uncle Sam perched in a tiny boat of his own and a puppeteer dressed in the dark suit of a businessperson carry signs that say, "Not me."

broken comms   *expletive deleted*
radio ID   uh sun as the sun's coming up hopefully you guys get a little
                                          (garble garble)

Your comms are weak and extremely broken uh understand we are still looking for
PID we are still eyes on the east side working on PID we have possible weapons but
no PID yet we'll keep you updated
                              Screener said at least one child near SUV

Bull *expletive deleted* Where!? Send me a *expletive deleted* still. I don't think
they have kids out at this hour I know they're shady but come on

                                                   At least one child

Really?   Listing the MAM uh that means he's guilty   Well maybe a teenager but
I haven't seen anything that looked that short granted they're all grouped up here but
    They're reviewing

                                          Yeah review that *expletive deleted*
Why didn't he say possible child why are they so quick to call *expletive deleted*
kids but not to call a *expletive deleted* rifle

                              Two children were at the rear of the SUV

                                   I haven't seen two children

So not likely to get any type of shot until they
have other asset to take the squirters or you know somehow divide and conquer
these vehicles
                                    If we had two missiles   Course now
we only have one   Little bit of movement by the SUV   I really doubt
that children call man I really *expletive deleted* hate that   Thanks dude

I don't think he's gonna let us shoot 'cause they wanna get all these guys but still
Maybe on a squirter   Yeah if we get this vehicle alone maybe but
no SUVs still trailing I think that truck well it's got everyone in the open so a
HELLFIRE would do dandy   A gas tank makes for a good secondary
too, hit a vehicle once before and it was a big black cloud

                                                    Yeah I think I saw that

The *expletive deleted* are they doing honestly?   Looks like both vehicles are
trying to slowly traverse this river *expletive deleted* it's up to   the   doors
They're getting their feet wet.   I hope they (expletive deleted) drown
them out man. Drown your *expletive deleted* out and wait to get shot
                                    It's getting up to the wheel wells
Alright so 1 2 3 4:30-5 in the morning trying to drive through a river with two
vehicles and pax everywhere,

                                                    Dude, call it.

I think they're gonna make it   I hope they get out and dry off and show us all
their weapons   Yeah exactly man   We   passed   him   potential
children and potential shields and I think those are both pretty accurate now what's
the ROE on that?

                                Ground commander assessing proportionality distinction
Is that part of CDE?   Is that part of ground command?   I'm not worried from
our stand point   so much, but that's a *expletive deleted* for them   I think
if that's the case and that's what they're confident with then they're gonna have to
wait until they start firing, 'cause then it essentially puts any possible civilian
casualties on the enemy but if we've got friendlies taking effective fire from that
position,

                                then we've gotta do what we gotta do

People fear that drones will be used indiscriminately, without conscience, without public consent, and (given their invisibility) without our knowledge, on anyone the state deems an enemy, even its own people. In the context of "homeland security," the fact that these are covert devices makes them categorically different from visible weapons. Nobody wants to see an armed helicopter hovering over their house, but if they do, at least the whole culture knows we're living in a police state. Without visibility, the safeguard of witnesses disappears. The stealth issue makes it harder to simply turn to the law because it is so much harder to know when it is being violated. Military ethicist Edward Barrett concedes, "These less visible weapons could facilitate the circumvention of legitimate authority and pursuit of unjust causes."[15]

While there will always be some people who care more about distant victims than others, everyone can share the fear that the kill chain will end with us, that we'll be haunted by the thought of the drone stationed above our city, the clicking bird filming us from the feeder, the moth on the screen door policing us, or the mosquito whose bite has injected who-knows-what into our bloodstreams. Will it genetically alter you and so, without your even knowing, you will no longer be yourself? Or will it simply kill you? When it comes to dissent, just the idea of such deadly puppets is a fierce ideological tool. In this world, we might need a theatre of invisible puppets whose presence is announced only by sound, unseen performance objects buzzing above our velvet seats, puppets to capture the feeling of surveillance, the feeling of terror.

Of course, the conversation about drones is also shaped by the fact that we live in a state committed to a doctrine of unending war and this constrains the ways in which we might legislate drone use. We can, and should, oppose any unethical use of "autonomous combat," any use that threatens to make us the puppets of the state, but until we can revive the notion of "peacetime" itself, all use is wartime use because all time is wartime.

Not bagpipe, sitar, or hurdy-gurdy. This drone sound is more like a motor. A sustained monotonous tone. A monophonic effect. A buzzing of male bees, eyes twice the size of workers', where MALE = Medium Altitude Long Endurance. Fly, hover, see. Fly, hover, see. Theirs is a machinic persistence. It gives them the ease of thoughtless determination. They've got the endless buzz of eternal war. One note continuously sounded.

We long for autonomy from danger, and in order to gain this, we cede our agency to others who will stand in our place, whether they are human soldiers or autonomous weapons systems. Inevitably, the desire for safety creates new dangers. It can be tempting to protect our security at any cost. But the cost of security can remake us. It can turn justified acts of defense into preemptive acts of tyranny. It can transform defenders into predators. We turn from the drone named Global Observer to the one we call the Predator. We turn from the Sentinel, Heron, and Hermes to the Hunter, Avenger, and Reaper. We turn from knowingly using these puppets as tools to numbly accepting the notion that the puppets themselves are in control. We watch them perform in scenes of declared combat like Afghanistan and then watch them re-stage in undeclared ones like Pakistan. Or Oakland. What would it take to turn this around? What Janus-faced puppet whose head can be spun to reveal that the backside of the demon is the god, that even situations that seem impossibly entrenched contain other possibilities? I'm not sure how moved I'd be by a Janus-puppet appearing in some old-time political street theatre intended to wake me up and get me moving. But what about Janus riding high on a citizen-deployed puppet- drone out to protect the people?

That papier mâché Uncle Sam puppet refusing the "all in the same boat" sentiment of the other paraders is a creation of the Bread and Puppet Theater. So much of my research has turned me toward their work, but I hesitate a long time before driving up to Vermont's Northeast Kingdom to visit them. I'm ambivalent; they are so old school. I find myself resisting their '70s hippie spectacle aesthetic and what I imagine will be a less than complex set of positions, and I find myself wishing they worked with a more contemporary medium and vocabulary. But they are so openly dedicated to anti-capitalism, and this radicalism appeals, so I feel compelled to take a look. I know it will be a long trip; nine hours on the road, and I'll have to sleep in the back of the car. When I say this to a friend, she points out that this is more choice than need since there are cheap hotels nearby, and that maybe my resistance to the hippie scene isn't as complete as I'd thought. And I do feel as though something is waiting for me there.

Evening gilds everything. Grass so green it is pink. The sun is setting on two huge barns. One houses fifty years worth of political puppets and the other is the Paper Maché Cathedral, home of Bread and Puppet's Dirt Floor Theater. It is tattooed with black hieroglyphs of human figures. Inside, the walls are frescoed with brown and black bas-relief papier mâché figures, patterns, and scenes. The lights go down. A voice says, "You are now in the real world, so don't do it if you aren't serious and I wish you to consider the cops and their tasers and their guns." The Uncle Sam puppet struts out onto the dirt floor of the stage only to be told, "The basic task of feet is kicking the ass of the government." A group of puppeteers yanks down his pants, leaving his pink cardboard buttocks exposed for their blows. The audience jeers happily but quiets down for "the elemental battle of good and evil." A group of players pantomime a vicious and deadly war while, behind them, a line of people in white shirts hum multiple melodies. It is painfully sad and beautiful. The white-clad singers slowly walk forward over the dead bodies, and it appears that they were "good" while the dead battlers were "evil," and that they have triumphed. But then they lie down with the dead. A long quiet. A pause. A thought.

Bread and Puppet founder Peter Schumann steps onto the balcony and says the bodies need to be addressed. He says "permanent impermanence." He says it is time to address stupidity and history with "the possibilitarian imperative to rise up to the post battle existence." He says, "The anti-disaster battle cry that life demands from us, the one the world demands from us, the one the world needs, is "Up and at 'em." The puppeteer Diggers exhort us to "stand up now."[16] They sing that "the gentry must come down and the poor shall wear the crown." The dead players rise and sing. And so does the watching crowd. Outrage and exhilaration.

While they make dinner, one young puppeteer says, "We're trying to articulate this world we're trying to build. You know the slogan 'There is another world'? We're trying to figure out what that can be, and a puppetry performance is an amazing entry point into further exploration of what kind of politics we want to have. Politics is about building a meaningful community and making our lives better. I think everyone wants to live in a world full of compassion, and friendship, and respect, and some measure of justice and fairness, but we tell ourselves that is impossible. You know that Howard Zinn quote 'You don't know what will happen if you do act, but you do know what will happen if you don't'? It is extraordinary to feel a call to make changes in your life, and then to work on how to live a life that is consistent with your belief system. On my best days, I feel that I am part of a history of people who have done their best to live with the contradictions and not let themselves off too easily."

I keep reading about puppets and run across some photographs of puppets on a float in the New York City May Day Parade of 1936. Fake ticker tape spewed, they said, like blood, covering "The Capitalist" puppet. His giant head stamped with a swastika. In Plate 11, Jackson Pollock descends the stairs, his hat pushed back on his head.[17] He guides a massive puppet limb down the face of the building. The fire escape trembles. He is perched outside the Siqueiros Experimental Workshop,

Mexican revolutionary muralist David Alfaro Siqueiros' 14th street studio where Pollock was a student. The hands of the gargantuan capitalist puppet they are building clutch both a donkey and an elephant. Relentlessly, a hammer and a sickle smash the ticker tape machine. Its streamers endlessly unfurling. Below, New York's Union Square was full of communists. Some say 60,000.

Eventually, I go back to Bread and Puppet several times. I take my children because I want to encourage their own possibilitarian impulses, because this is what I love about them, because this is what I'm longing for, and because of the high clouds and the sweet fierce people there. One day, watching the puppeteers parade by on stilts waving little wooden fighter jets and paper daffodils in the air, I find myself raising an eyebrow once again at their old-school stylings. I'm a little embarrassed to be here, but also deeply happy and at home. It's a fucked up feeling, but nice in the way it keeps me close to contradiction, the only truth I think I can know. And really, I kind of wish I could join them. Suddenly, one of the puppeteers breaks from the pack and stalks toward my children and I, calling my name and my older son's name as well. I am disoriented until I realize she is a former student of mine who is now at school with my son. I ask her what she's doing here, and she laughs and smiles and sways her body above us on her tall stilts and zooms her toy jet toward our heads and shrugs as if to say, "Isn't it obvious?" and begins to sing along with an accordion player who is now walking past. She waves and glides back to her troupe as they approach the center of town where the sidewalks are speckled with people on lawn chairs. One older woman says, "Well, what's all this about?" and a puppeteer stops to tell her about their opposition to an F-35 fighter base the military has proposed to open in a residential neighborhood in Burlington.

One day, the news is full of reports on protests in France; people are opposing the government's proposal to raise the retirement age. Labor unions have blockaded a major refinery, and truck drivers are employing "escargot," or snail operation, to slow their rigs to a crawl. In one picture, protesters gathered in the streets of Paris use long bamboo poles to loft an enormous puppet-woman dressed in a long white dress into the air. There is blood on her face. Behind her, more people carry a tall replica of the scales of justice. The caption says that the puppeteers are members of the Théâtre du Soleil, a company run without hierarchies where the members live communally, work collaboratively, are paid equal wages, and share meals with their audiences. "Théâtre du Soleil is the dream of living, working, being happy and searching for beauty and for goodness. . . . It's trying to live for higher purposes, not for richness,"[18] says founder and director Ariane Mnouchkine. "We are on the path to utopia. I accept that."[19]

Theatre du Soleil's productions are often called antiestablishment, or progressive, and frequently include the use of puppets. Mnouchkine follows Artaud's ideas about the theatrical power of "animated hieroglyphs" (made visible by Balinese dancers for Artaud) in the form of actors who are able to distil something conceptual into a physical form, actors who can produce a sense of "matter as revelation" as Artaud wrote. Mnouchkine's production of Hélène Cixous' play "Tambours sur la Digue," or "Drums on the Dam: In the Form of an Ancient Puppet Play Performed by Actors,"[20] offers an uncanny encounter with actors dressed as Bunraku puppets, their faces immobile masks. These actors are manipulated by other actors dressed as traditional Japanese puppeteers, the kuroko or "black robes" of nothingness. Mnouchkine says, "Being a puppet offers a wider field of expression that is otherwise unavailable to human actors. It is more hidden, more subtle, more difficult in a way. But being a marionette gives you the opportunity to signal almost everything, and if you are able to do this, there are no limits." Cixous takes this a step further, saying all theatre is puppetry ("toute est marionettes").

The narrative of the play reveals how the central characters are powerless in the face of both natural and political devastation; in the production, the actors are powerless to move their own bodies. Thus, says Cixous, the puppets are "the externalization of the interior puppet which we are." In his review of the play, Ron Jenkins tells how "a similar transference of human qualities to inanimate objects occurs during the play's final scene in which the flood finally annihilates all life in the kingdom." He explains,

> The stage's central platform is removed to reveal the body of water that it was feared would one day engulf the kingdom. Tiny puppets, with the faces and costumes of each character, are then hurled into the water in a miniaturized massacre that has the paradoxical effect of making the deaths seem larger than life.
>
> In the end, the only human presence on the stage is a puppet master who wades through the water to retrieve the small puppets and line them up to dry on the edge of the stage. His watery ritual of rescue is mesmerizing. The collection of puppet faces matches the characters that the audience has come to know, and their limp helplessness is wrenching. . . . when the characters who have been acting like puppets all through the play are suddenly transformed into real puppets, the audience's suspension of disbelief is jolted into a state of hyper-awareness that may lead spectators to reflect on the necessity of creating fictions to evoke the memory of real events.[21]

Mnouchkine comments on these final scenes, saying, "Even in the worst tragedy you always have a few people who are there trying to save what there is to be saved. And for me, the puppeteer at that moment is simply trying to save what little there is to be saved, which is the possibility of telling their story again. What he is saving is not the people, because they are dead. But the puppeteer saves the possibility of continuing to tell their story, which is also important. It's not a resurrection of the characters. It is a resurrection of their memories." For Mnouchkine and other political puppetry theaters, the resurrection is almost always one of memory, of commitment, of struggle, or reparation. The theater, Mnouchkine says, wants "to reinvent the rules of the game which reveal daily reality, showing it not to be familiar and immutable, but astonishing and transformable."[22]

[Breathing covers dialogue]

weather right now

Roger

Why all these puppets? Bread and Puppet Theater's Peter Schumann says, "People exist as citizens and puppets are insurrectionists and therefore shunned by correct citizens—unless they pretend to be something other than what they are, like fluffy, lovely or digestible." Whether the puppet is our tool or our toy, puppets are political because they wear on their faces our own lack of power and our desire for it. Puppets perform our longing for autonomy and its absence—in love, in work, in affairs of state. When the wooden head turns to look at you, the gesture is intimate, real. It stirs you more than the real gestures of the audience all around you. Puppets offer us a way to see ourselves; like us, they are at once actors and acted upon. Puppets are both objects and subjects blind to their constitutive subjectivity, just as we so often are. Puppets concretize our social relations, and in making this visible, maybe the normally abstract forces that limit us can also be concretized, seen, understood and, hence, possibly overcome.[23] In the object of the puppet, we glimpse the subject of the human. In the object of the drone, we glimpse the subject of society.

And when we say children are we talking teenagers or toddlers   I would
say about twelve   Not toddlers   Something more towards adolescents or
teens   Yeah adolescents   Looks to be potential adolescents
We're thinking early teens   Screener agrees   Adolescents
Good copy on that   We are with you   Our screener updated only one
adolescent so that's one double digit age range   How Copy?   We'll pass
that along to the ground force commander   But
like I said 12-13 years old with a weapon is just as dangerous   Oh we agree
Yeah   Good copy on that   We understand and agree
They're saying yep we got PID we just wanna see where they're goin'

As long as you keep somebody that we can shoot in the field of view I'm happy

                                                                    Roger that

Yeah they're trying to confirm which vehicle has the kids in it oh the adolescents in it
Who is?   SOTF South   Screener is talking about it right now
Okay   But JTAC already said that well they can grab a gun so   Hey   you
know what those mujadeen 13 years old   Yeah, well that's what
we were talking on this I was talking to the JTAC he said the exact same thing man
um they called them an adolescent we called it you know most likely double digits
age range and he was like that's old enough to be dangerous   Yep
Which is true I mean he was helping them load stuff earlier.   DGS called it
out. Helping load things into a back of a truck when we first got on station that's
when that AC130 was like please give me PID

                              I was like   we can't

It's a cool looking shot							O awesome

Break um understand we are clear to engage   Okay he's clear to engage
I'm going to spin our missiles up as well   Roger that   Uh okay Bam Bam
41 will be uh turning in to engage will call back with the BDA   Let the SMIC
know   Do you have uh do you have the previous freq for uh *expletive
deleted*   Jag there MC?   I do   CLASSIFIED

CLASSIFIED

                              And you might want to call for a safety observer

                                                                              Yeah

Hamid Kharzai: "Well, me a puppet. (Closes eyes.) My God. Anyway, Americans have helped Afghanistan tremendously. The American people have a feeling for Afghanistan. For which we are very, very grateful. The U.S. administration has helped Afghanistan. And if we are called puppets or if I'm called a puppet because we are grateful to America then, (hand gesture), so be it. Let that be my nickname. The truth is that without United States' support of Afghanistan, Afghanistan would have been a very poor, miserable country occupied by neighbors and by Al-Quaida and the terrorists. Whoever is elected by the American people will be our best ally. (Smiles.)"[24]

In her book *War at a Distance; Romanticism and the Making of Modern War,* Mary A. Favret traces how, with the rise of distant wars at the end of the eighteenth century, the ways in which "time and knowledge were registered in daily life became newly uncertain. And with that uncertainty came a set of disturbing affective responses including numbness, dizziness, anxiety, or a sense of being overwhelmed." Favret's exploration of the ways in which Romantic writers are the "architects of modern wartime," reveals a foundational moment in the "relations of distance, temporality, epistemology, and affect: the felt distance from crucial events, the limits of knowledge in a mediated culture, the temporal gaps in the transmission of information, and, finally, the difficulty of finding sounds or forms to which feeling can attach itself."[25]

"Finding sounds or forms to which feeling can attach itself." Maybe this is what I want from puppets.

I am watching Pina Bausch. The sensation she induces relies on a puppet modality—patently false and achingly intimate. Her exaggerated and tiresome gestures carry an ache that makes me want to dance inside her body while she choreographs an emotion (her cigarette her prop, the condensation of her character). As a dancer, when she enters, she is a puppet. Watch the puppet Pina glide on stage; it is stunningly like her. At once lithe and awkward, bony and graceful, the puppet Pina begins to dance her "Cafe Müller" (1978). The skeletal, nightgowned marionette with her startling rib cage and thin, drooping breasts looks half-dead. Sleepwalking, she shuffles forward, eyes closed, long hair trailing, arms outstretched, palms up, hands low, just in front of her hollow pelvis. Her arms are weirdly long. Especially the forearms—like a praying mantis with elongated sticks—radius and ulna stretched out in front of her. She is reaching for something. A descending chromatic line enters; a passus duriusculus. Suffered hard. Harsh passage. 3/2 time. G-minor. The puppet's arms lower and seem to soften just as the aria becomes familiar. When I am laid, am laid in earth. "Dido's Lament." Aeneas has betrayed and abandoned Dido. There is despair, and, why not death? You left me. I can't bear it. The song is a wedge. It pries something open.

The puppet's arms swoop back outstretched from her sides like wings, then fling behind the clearly articulated vertebrae of her spine. She arches, her bony chest thrust forward in a gesture of longing. Her hands sweep upward to the sky and her joints lock. At the top of the arc, her body collapses forward, crushed in a deep bow. Elbows bent; arms a box. Then one arm swings fluidly out and up, followed by the other swirling like a ribbon in the air. An expression of pained concentration is drawn on her face—a flamenco frown, though not as fierce. But still, so sad. *May my wrongs create no trouble, no trouble, in thy breast.*

Rocking and bending, the Pina puppet's body straightens and stumbles forward haltingly. The aria swells again. Rising and dropping. The puppet uses her right hand to push her left arm away, again and again.

A compulsive repetition. The woman sitting next to me in the audience begins to cry. Downstage, someone is furiously crashing into tables and knocking over chairs. Someone else races to save him from harm and to pick up after him. Tailing them, a woman with flaming hair and a coat like a bear's teeters in a pair of red high heels. Her costume turns her, too, into a clumsy puppet. She looks like she wants to help, but doesn't know how. She skitters helplessly back and forth. There is nothing anyone can do. The raging man writhing in the foreground has become a projection of something inside the Pina figure rather than a being with whom she is in relation. He flails on the floor. Frustration and futility; longing, destruction, and sorrow. This is how love puppets us. And abandonment. Or betrayal.

Remember me, Dido sings. I'm still here. Every day, the sleepwalking of loving someone who has already sailed. She can't stop saying his name. Aeneas, Aeneas, Aeneas. The way it feels in her mouth when she is walking in the street, when she is lying in the bath. She circles around his name, tethered. In love, we feel ourselves come alive, become real. In love, we believe that only with our love are we fully ourselves. If betrayed, we become the puppet of two masters: the betrayer and the new love. They can control us. Destroy us. Dido falls to the floor. Dead, her feet slung at an impossible angle; they seem more like organs than limbs. And in that moment, a memory interrupts, a memory of looking down from a pew in the visitors' balcony of the monastery in Gethsemene, Kentucky, looking down at another pair of feet at exactly the same miserable angle. The brown-shoed feet of a dead monk in an open casket, his few remaining brothers in the dwindling order singing beside him. Both a life and way of living can die. Dido is dead, the monk is dead, our love is dead, and Pina Bausch is dead. The puppet is not dead.

The words *articulate* and *articulation* jump up from the jointed puppet. The first usage example is from Crooke's 1615 *Microcosmographia.* It says, "Almost every articulation is crusted over with a gristle to make the motion more easie, more secure and more permanent." What gristle encrusts the articulations that make emotion "more easier, more secure, and more permanent"? The second usage of articulation is from William Derham's 1713 *Physico-Theology*. The quote here says, "the finest Articulations, and Foldings, for the Wings to be withdrawn, and neatly laid up in their Vaginæ and Cases." Vaginae? Plural? Unexpected. But here Pina Bausch suddenly appears again, wings folding to be withdrawn into her vaginae, a reverse metamorphosis to mirror her transmogrification from human to embodied feeling. The final usage example I find for articulation reads: "The manifestation, demonstration, or expression of something immaterial or abstract, such as an emotion or idea."

"In using puppets with Army men in an understanding of psychoneurosis, puppets make real such emotions as resentment, fear, anger, and sorrow; that is, they present convincingly the fact that these abstractions really exist. . . . Lieutenant Colonel R. Robert Cohen has supervised the use of puppets for the retraining of psychoneurotics at the Aberdeen Proving Ground. A number of visual aids are used in group therapy; the puppet show is regarded as one of the best, because it has concreteness, humor, and movement. Colonel Cohen says: 'Puppets are admirably suited to presenting a basic understanding of human emotions to the average soldier, because a puppet as a symbolic character can easily project an abstract idea which, a human actor would find difficult and involved. In effect, the puppet is a three-dimensional presentation of an otherwise abstract concept."

—Marjorie Batchelder, *The Puppet Theatre Handbook.*[26]

(Batchelder was a major American puppeteer and a leading developer of the hand-rod puppet style later used by Jim Henson.)

Why puppets? Because after everything else, they are a relief—cattails of rotting velvet bobbing on wands and bursting into lofting fluff. Because they are amusing to look at, like stars. Because, like us, they are moved by others. Because the triangle of forces on which their stage is built is easily recognized: Side A: The desire to make something happen (puppeteer), Side B: The comfort of just being moved along, surrendering control (puppet), Side C: The pleasure of watching and of submitting to an illusion (spectator). Pulling, being pulled, and watching. Agency, passivity, spectatorship. Subject, object, witness. Because inertia, not love, is like oxygen. Poor puppets, so pathetic and familiar. Easy to deride, but sneaky and latent because they marry disenchantment and its reversal. They're made of disappointment, insomnia, and signal. Inert, they gesture. I am embarrassed, entranced, elated. Puppets can be an animating spectacle.

Then again, maybe now, cheered, we won't do anything. But this is also an old story. Rancière summarizes the problem of passive spectatorship that Brecht and Artaud struggled against by saying, "To be a spectator is to be separated from both the capacity to know and the power to act."[27]

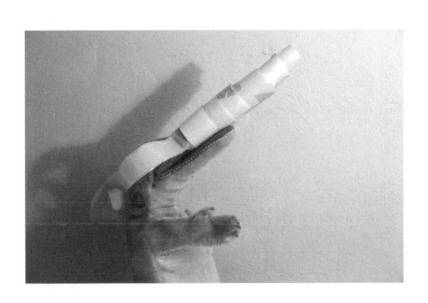

Like the audience, the puppet, too, is separated from the capacity to know and the power to act, but unlike the audience, the puppet acts anyway. I've been avoiding Pinocchio, but here he is. The puppet without strings. Although he makes his own decisions and moves according to some internal force, this is not enough for him to be considered human; he is still merely a puppet. Scholar Suzanne Stewart-Steinberg argues that Pinocchio's confusing relationship to autonomy is a site where ideas about an Italian national self and subject were explored and developed in the late nineteenth century, and, in fact, critics often read Pinocchio as a model for the citizen-subject who is drawn to the freedom of personal adventure but must learn the pleasures of responsibility, attachment, and commitment. Conservative screed or a validation of love as a communitarian force?

Pinocchio longs to be free to do what he wants. To be independent. He wants the autonomy to follow his desires. I once saw a Pinocchio puppet whose inflatable rubber nose went flaccid, then rigid, every time he lied. Because, of course, you know it's not just his nose that grows, but, well, his will. Wood was always part of the story. He leads with his desire. He doesn't want to be a spectator of life; he wants to act. And so he's off. He runs. But his freedom to roam and do as he likes is always followed by trouble, suffering, and hunger. Then, a competing desire nips him, the desire to be free from pain, from want. The desire to be able to take care of himself and his family. To be responsible. To gain a different kind of independence. He is a puppet pulled between two mastering desires. He tries to be good. But he hates the drudgery of work. Hates school. Hates to be obedient. And there is always some temptation. Some distracting puppet theatre full of his brothers-in-wood (*fratelli-di-legno*) drinking beer and partying. The possibility of living in Funland without doing his hateful job. Why would he stay? For his family, he remembers. Then runs. He's a recidivist. An addict. In Collodi's original story, when the cricket of conscience just won't shut up and leave him be, Pinocchio smashes it dead with a mallet. He wants to do the right thing, but it is just so hard. He's a bad boy. But we love him anyway.

On the run, Pinocchio meets a beautiful girl with turquoise hair, sky-blue hair (*capelli turchini, color del cielo*), blue like the Madonna's veil, her breasts milky bluish-white with veins like distant water. She is nursing, nurturing, and alluring. She is the azure fairy who saves him from his pursuers; together, she and Pinocchio are happy. For a while. Soon, he gets restless and leaves the blue fairy of love behind. One day, wandering, he stumbles across a gravestone. It reads: "Here lies the girl with the blue hair who died of grief for having been abandoned by her Pinocchio." He cries bitterly and says, "If you love me, come back. I am alone and I want to die." *Voglio morire,* Collodi writes. But she doesn't come back and he will only ever see her again in his dreams where he feels her just as he did at the beginning, small, pale, and dear. Pinocchio's lost love and his shame at killing it lead him to change his ways, and he begins to find pleasure in working to provide for his father, his family. His genuine turn to the satisfaction of caretaking frees him from being a puppet and allows him to become fully human. In a dream, the girl with the sky-blue hair returns and transforms him. He wakes to see his former puppet self slouched in the corner and says what a clown he was and how glad he is to be a good boy now. He turns the wooden puppet around and paints its back with pictures of the past. He is resolute. It is time to grow up. It seems like a happy ending, but, even though we felt the killing pain of his lies, it is hard not to feel a creeping nostalgia for the puppet who was so much freer than the boy, so much more autonomous and alive. The puppet can be a tricky figure.

According to the logic of Collodi's Pinocchio, what makes us human is turning our drive for pleasure into responsible love and a curbing of selfishness. Like Pinocchio, I feel myself rankle and squirm at this and want to reinterpret his story so the turn to responsibility is not quite so conformist a turn toward familial duty and obedience to the state. I'd like to move forward under Pinocchio's banner, under the sign of the lying, cheating, scoundrel with a healthy disregard for work whose trajectory moves from betrayal to shame to responsibility to action. But, really, I think I'd rather have the betrayed Blue Fairy as my standard or on my coat-of-arms. I'm stuck on her. I'm stuck on her as I'm stuck on love and even on betrayal—maybe because betrayal more nearly captures my experience of powerlessness and its possible, but difficult, reversals.

A dream of words. Butterfly, mariposa, amapola, poppies, opium, Pasiphae. Typed white on black. Married to Minos but cursed by Poseidon, Pasiphae longed for some white bull she couldn't have, until Daedalus built her a contraption—better than wings—a wooden cow costume, a wearable, jointed puppet. A Trojan horse for sex in which the Minotaur was conceived. A puppet for love.

The letters in the dream turn you toward the bull. See the bull. So white. So massive. He's breathtaking. In some dim frieze, you've seen the bullock's buttocks. Then, the roundness of *her* ass. The pale yellow-white marble. Anticipation of the adjacent topography. Look at her finger. The hand goes higher. Other geometries emerge. Fur gives presence to fragments. Fetishes. Stop getting between me and my language. That tattoo is called a stripper tail. Look at her watching him. Later, she'll think how heavy he was. His laugh, a warm breath in the grass. Some rich person's lawn where he peed gallons.

To want it. To do anything for it. The secret paleness, the nonchalance of animality, the void. Pacify means put it in your mouth and suck on it. But nothing pacifies me now.

In Hugh Lloyd Jones' translation of Euripides' *Cretans,* Pasiphae says:

> It makes no sense; what is it about the bull that could have stirred up such a shameful passion? It can hardly have been some symmetry of form! This is the love for which I got into the skin and went on all fours.

Some passions make no sense. Some passions shame us. The ones that pull us. Like her namesake, Pasiphae, the moon of Jupiter, an amber satellite circling in endless attraction. The ones for which we get on all fours. The ones for which we'll put on the cow suit. Or the human suit. Get into the skin. Puppet ourselves.

He writes of his dream: We were going to miss each other by being in certain places at almost, but not quite, the same time. At one point, your presence was so strongly implied that I could see you nearby in a beam of sunlight, or nearly, as if you had just left. I gradually came to understand that I could learn to communicate with you by means of some oversize kitchen sponges, three-foot rectangles of foam, one sky blue, the other pale yellow the color of chamois or hide. Another dream, the end of dreams. We were trying to place two rectangular signs on the back window of a sedan. One said TRAUMA and the other said DRAMA. The Greek roots differ. Trauma is to wound or to pierce. Drama is to act or to do. To do it. In the dream, we were trying to figure out, by placing the signs of trauma and drama on top of each other, if they were the exact same size and thus, by extension, the exact same thing.

Hidden here: the scene on the other side of the phone. What you can hear is him careening around his apartment knocking over bottles. Hear them crashing. Think: bull in a china shop. Think: here is someone observing the schedule of harm. Abasement. One word. A basement. Two words. Go down. Darts. Cowhide rugs. Go down. The word *cattle* did not originate as a name for bovine animals. It derives from the Latin word. *Caput.* Head. Jackson Pollock's painting of Pasiphae and the bull was in his first one-man show in 1943. The painting was originally called *Moby Dick.*

Did you know that yoked oxen cannot slow a load like harnessed horses can; the load has to be controlled on the incline. From here, things go downhill. I can't stop myself. I am out of control. I am controlled only by my longing and can't hear *no,* can't hear *stop.* I wear the cow suit constantly. For a long time, the shame is no match for the dopamine lining of this puppet. But it would have been better to refuse its seductive technology, because the tale ends badly. Pasiphae reports: "My baby has his father's head." Deadly, he must live in a maze of punishment patterned on the River Maeander that flows both backward and forward. A confusion more tidal zone than tributary loops across the territory. In the end, the moral of the story clearly places fidelity over falsehood.

"Maybe we're here in order to experience people as a reason for love," or maybe we exist in order to feel shame: "Shame—the feeling that will save mankind." These are the speculations of the astronaut-psychologist Kris Kelvin in Tarkovsky's *Solaris.* Like Pinocchio, Kris has his Blue Fairy, Hari. Her blue lips. Her blue paper gown. Her skin filmed with ice. She has that fairy glamour (glamour, a variant of grammar derived from the occult practices of learning) being magically made from "a transcription of a thought." Like the Blue Fairy, she too is betrayed. She too dies of heartbreak. And as with Pinocchio, we are asked to consider that Kris might be saved by his shame, even as both stories end with a sense of doomed enclosure wherein the power of their acting with personal responsibility is thrown into question by the pervasive and rigid containing systems of their worlds. Both stories' ostensible valorization of individual agency is further undermined by the fact that these narratives share, as Stewart-Steinberg writes of *Pinocchio,* a view of love as "linked to a subject whose space is assumed to be autonomous, independent, and private."[28] What if love were reconfigured as both private and public, both independent and dependent, or even simultaneously interior and communal?

The world of *Solaris* is intensely private, intensely focused on the individual's interior life. The scientists on the space station have given up their research in favor of working with their personal demons, their pasts, their memories. Hari, made solely from Kris' memories, has none of her own, and is thus deprived of any autonomy. Being simply a part of Kris' past makes her his puppet. She is a being with no sense of self beyond her slowly growing recollections of love, betrayal, despair, and death, and without any further knowledge, she doesn't know how to act. Learning her past gives her more human feelings, but what she learns is that she is not human and that she is powerless, powerless against the pain of his betrayals and against the pain of living. We watch as she realizes that when he said he loved her, he was loving someone else. We watch as everything she encounters reminds her of the other woman and his love for her. We watch as she is controlled by these feelings and he feels controlled by her. They aren't struggling *for* power, but under it. But Kris is also a puppet, a puppet to the planet's sea of consciousness which has more agency than the visiting humans. He is powerless against the eternal returns of his daughter-wife-mother, and her shame-inducing unconditional love. Later, his feelings shift and he confesses that he didn't love her when she was human, but does so now. It is hard to know how to feel about this. Do we experience sympathy for his discovery of love or suspicion that he loves her now because she is more a part of himself than an autonomous being, more object than subject? Then again, one might ask, what's wrong with loving a thing, or being one?

In the film, Hari is so powerless, she can't even end her suffering by ending her own life. When she kills herself, she is doomed to be born again only as a part of Kris. After each death, her eyes open, staring, lifelike, like a doll or a puppet we know will be reanimated. With a shudder, she melts and is reborn. She has the Blue Fairy's sad gift of parthenogenesis, the puppet's gift for resurrection. It hurts right away. He holds her. The doctor says it will get worse. "The more she's with you, the more human she'll become." But she will always know that she's also not quite human. Her suffering is the type defined by Adorno when he writes, "Suffering is objectivity that weighs upon the subject." Hari suffers, as we all do, when we feel ourselves to be objects or when we are treated as objects.

Hey MC   Yes?   Remember Killchain!   Will   do   (Unintelligible)
Killchain   Will do will do will do   The only two things that ever get briefed in
the in the shot brief (laughter)   You'll be alright on this pass I'll uh re-center you
and uh   Roger and oh!   and   there   it   goes!
(unintelligible)   Our engagement   It was backing up   Stand by

Have another guy did they get him too?   Yep

They took the first and uh the last out   They're going to come back around

I see squirters at the first one   Yep

Your call, sir   Uh, follow what you think
makes the most sense in fact, stay on the middle truck for now   I will
Until they take that out or we do

               Do we want to switch back to other frequency?
                         I tried, nobody was talking to me over there

Looks like they're surrendering

                                              They're not running

CLASSIFIED [NOTE: At this point additional voices appear on the recording—
presumably those of the safety observers—and identifying which individual is
speaking at any given time becomes very difficult.]

You got a mountain coming into view

Keep it a turn   Copy   Rog thanks   Copy the turn   In the turn
(unintelligible, middle vehicle is struck by missile) set you up   Oh!
Rog there it is   Alright, follow, uh,   whatever you think makes sense man

That guy's laid down?   They're not running   Dude, this is weird
They're just walking away   I think I've got the bulk of whoever's left in the
field of view   Yeah, I think so   You want to see if there's anybody at
the back?   Yeah (unintelligible) outline   By that third wreck   A
couple—two or three

Yeah, they're just chilling

Zoom in on that for a second for me the third one   The third one?   Yeah did
they blow that up they did, right   They did, yeah   No they didn't   They
didn't   They didn't   No, they're just out there   Yeah, that thing looks
destroyed, though, doesn't it?   Yeah they hit it there's some smoke

They hit it

These guys are just   (rocket attack on middle vehicle)   Oh!   Holy
expletive deleted   I don't know about this this is weird.   Yeah
Got nowhere to go   Probably confused as *expletive deleted*   Oh   yeah,
they just got thrown from the vehicle, too   We did call we did tell them
there was adolescents in the second vehicle so I thought that was the reason they
didn't shoot the (unintelligible) second vehicle   No   No   I doubt it
I know   Nobody is talking to me   That's weird
Can't tell what the *expletive deleted* they're doing   Probably wondering
what happened   There's one more to the left of the screen   Yeah I see them

                        Are they wearing burqas?

That's what it looks like   They were all PIDed as males though   No females in
the group   That guy looks like he's wearing jewelry and stuff like a girl
but he ain't   If he's a girl he's a big one   Bam   Bam   uh   we   are
eyes on the squirters at this time   No weapons PIDed yet

You're headed outbound pretty quick   (unintelligible)

The constant drone of drones. The constant drone of systems. The constant drone of relational navigations. Bodies, doxa, love, annihilation. The soundtrack is drone music. Only those driving overtones and undertones can match the steady ferocity of the stalking machine, the ceaseless intensity of our prosaic contradictions, and the duality of narcosis and heightened awareness they induce. The trace of chant and trance. The bagpipes of war and the ragas of transcendence.

Drone music has only slight harmonic variations from a central, sustained tonality around which the rest of the composition builds—a kind of constant buzz or thrum within the music. Monks chanting, the organ in the cathedral, South Asian monophonic music played over a constant drone whether with drone instruments like the tambura, the dotara, the shank or conch shell, or with instruments that contain a drone element: the sitar, sarod, and rudra veena—sounds that resurface in the music of La Monte Young and Pandit Pran Nath, Henry Flynt, Alice Coltrane, the Velvet Underground, Sunn O))). Listen. What is the resonance of their sonic landscapes here? Does the relationship of all the drones we know reach beyond the homonymic?

In his essay "The Eternal Drone," Marcus Boon writes, "In India, one way of saying drone is 'Nada Brahma'—'God is sound,' or 'sound is God,'" and in his exploration of what Indian musician and philosopher Sufi Hazrat Inayat Khan calls "the music of the Absolute" with its continuous bass, Boon reminds us that "the traditional name given to this never-ending undertone, which has been repeated by musicians from Coltrane and Can to Anti-Pop Consortium, is OM, and by saying OM, the monk or the musician tunes into perfect sound forever." Drone music often accompanies ceremonial or ritual enactments, the purpose of which is to relieve the listener of "autonomy," that is to turn one into a puppet or vessel for transcendence. However, as Boon is quick to point out, "Like all former sacred technologies in the modern era, including drugs, dance and ritual, erotic play or asceticism, musicians have appropriated and reconfigured the drone's power in many ways that question traditional notions of the sacred. . . . In fact the drone is a perfect vehicle for expressing alienation from conventional notions of the sacred."[29] Whether tonally dark or light, drone music is still a channel for being occupied, controlled, released, or ventriloquized by an outside force.

What's that?

What'd you say?

Wow   (unintelligible)   That   truck   is   so   dead   Wow

The thing is nobody ran   Yeah that was weird   So all the squirters
have returned to the road at this point   Yeah   *Expletive deleted* how can
we have good comms for four hours straight   (unintelligible)
                                    was cut short although it is damaged
uh estimate four five individuals from the lead vehicle got out uh a couple from the
trail vehicle although they appear to be uh not moving very much   at all

Came in extremely broken   *Broken Transmission*

        Yeah I see what you're saying there's his head

We are still searching   Yeah see there's that guy just sat up
                                                                              Yeah

        So it looks like those lumps are probably all people

                                                                              Yep

When Adorno wrote that "suffering is objectivity that weighs upon the subject," he concluded that "the need to let suffering speak is a condition of all truth."

Attacked, defeated, beaten, abused, exploited, suffering, we become someone's, or something's, puppet, pawn, or object. The real puppet, although it is always strung up, always exploited, and often beaten, remains expressive throughout its suffering. It is this fettered expressiveness that is so touching and that seems to offer us some truth. In his "Note on Puppets," George Bernard Shaw wrote, "I always hold up the wooden actors as instructive object-lessons to our flesh-and-blood players." Shaw says that "the wooden ones, though stiff and continually glaring at you with the same overcharged expression, yet move you as only the most experienced living actors can" and adds that few actors can achieve the intensity found in the puppet's "unchanging stare, petrified (or rather lignified) in a grimace expressive to the highest degree attainable by the carver's art," or in "the mimicry by which it suggests human gesture in unearthly caricature."[30]

The puppet bows its head when it is hung on a nail and again when it takes the stage. The puppet raises its chin, walks jerkily at first, then lifts off the ground a little, finds its center of gravity, and comes alive. The torso angles just so, the head tilts, the arm lowers slightly. It is at once awkward and graceful. When the wooden head turns to look at you, the gesture is intimate, real. It stirs you more than the real gestures of the audience all around you. It is a thing and a thing in itself. Dead and alive. Forced to obey and independent. Immune to suffering, it suffers. It convinces us of its pain through its implausible grace. Grace. Both a fluid movement and a divine mercy. The word derives from the Greek *charis,* the root of charisma, character, and effortless charm. In Heinrich von Kleist's famous essay "On the Marionette Theatre," he tells of a dancer who claimed that "Where grace is concerned, it is impossible for man to come anywhere near a puppet. Only a god can equal inanimate matter in this respect. This is the point where the two ends of the circular world meet." The point where the two ends of the circular world meet. The god and the puppet. The divine and the inanimate. The all-powerful and the powerless.

Von Kleist's dancer explains,

> Just as a section drawn through two lines suddenly reappears on the other side after passing though infinity, or as the image in a concave mirror turns up again right in front of us after dwindling into the distance, so grace itself returns where knowledge has, as it were, gone through an infinity. Grace appears most purely in that human form which either has no consciousness or an infinite consciousness. That is, in the puppet or the god.[31]

Two kinds of grace shimmer here: the physical and spiritual. For Von Kleist, physical grace is found both through the single point of gravity that animates the puppet's simple gestures (so unlike the disorder of human movement) and through an absence of affectation that can only be achieved through a lack of self-consciousness, especially the absence of human embarrassment at one's own individuality, one's separateness from the world. "Man," Von Kleist writes, "is a creature permanently off balance." This is the link to the second kind of grace that concerns Von Kleist, the spiritual one we have fallen from, the place of innocence and lack of consciousness we cannot return to, but can only hope to move toward, paradoxically, by moving toward infinite knowledge and consciousness. As an agnostic, the idea of divine grace carries only a little glimmer for me, but if grace can be re-imagined as the undeserved mercy we show each other in our attempts to alleviate suffering, then the glimmer brightens. Von Kleist looked to the poles, pure consciousness and no consciousness, but what they illuminate is what lies in between: human consciousness, human mercy, and a human grace. In considering the poles, what fascinated Von Kleist was what he called "the paradox" and what his dancer called "the contradictions." This is because in a paradox, two conflicting truths can both be valid, and in the impossible space of that tension, we glimpse something glowing.

For Adorno, to think in contradictions, to think against thought, is the only route to exposing the antagonisms of our world in order to reach for possible resolutions. This thinking in contradiction is based in a utopian impulse to open a route beyond our domination of nature, of each other, and of "difference," so that we might find some reconciliation, some grace, some experience that might actually exceed the grasp of thought. Adorno calls this "das Nichtidentische." The Nonidentical. Can puppets—in their performance of the contradictions of their own existence, their own impossible yet convincing subjectivity, their paradoxical appearance as both subjects and objects—offer us a glimpse of this experience that exceeds the grasp of thought? Perhaps puppets are a figure of the non-identical of the human (or the animal, the animate), in other words, the speculative identity between thought and being, between subject and object. Puppets can thus embody a utopian mode of thinking whose significance is the possible alleviation of the suffering.

When Adorno spoke of "the need to let suffering speak is a condition of all truth," one of the truths he sought was that of art, particularly the way art can challenge actual social conditions without becoming utilitarian propaganda. In other words, he sought an art that maintains the autonomy of its purposelessness without being irrelevant to social transformation.

A banner on the side of the barn at the Bread and Puppet Theater reads: "Irrelevanting toward irrelevancy."

One of Adorno's favorite practitioners of letting suffering speak, of an art that becomes political by exposing the contradictions of society, was Samuel Beckett (to whom Adorno had intended to dedicate his *Aesthetic Theory*), who had the knack of turning his players into suffering puppets caught between humiliation and grace. In fact, Beckett frequently spoke of his characters as puppets and, when working with actors, often referred them to one of his favorite essays: Von Kleist's "On the Marionette Theatre."

Two strategies Adorno identifies as necessary to realize the truth of art and to "unleash the history on the object":

1. The use of the "expressive" dimensions of language, as opposed to the sanctioned syntax and semantics of the everyday
2. The removal of established concepts from their habitual patterns by placing them in "constellations" around a certain topic[32]

CLASSIFIED   Correct   And Jag25   Jag25   Jag25   Kirk97 on Purple26

They're trying to *explicative* surrender right?

            I think

                        That's what it looks like to me

                                    Yeah I think that's what they're doing

He's calling females?   They said 21 males no females   Earlier yeah   Now
they're calling 3 females and 1 child 1 possible child   Called him a adolescent
earlier   Should probably pass that while Bam's on station Or pass it to Jag

Yeah but I can't get ahold of Jaguar right now

                                                                I'd tell him they're waving their

I get a text from my brother who has recently retired from the military and is back in a plane flying for a contractor somewhere over Africa. I try to look away from the reality of this. He is thinking of extending his stay there but wants to confirm the date of my visit so he can be back in time. I feel a lick of guilt since I have been thinking that maybe this visit I might finally get up the nerve to ask him some more difficult questions about his work. But I don't want to ambush him. He's my only sibling, and we grew up with no relatives in the United States, just the two of us and our parents. It's funny, we weren't really that close as children, and I have vivid memories of our chronic fights, but somehow I've succumbed to the allure of family relations—a dominion both saccharine and truly sweet.

Recently, I had coffee with a friend and she mentioned that her brother makes the surveillance equipment my brother employed. She says that she has only just realized the implications of this and doesn't want to know much more because, as she says, "I just want to be able to sit on the couch and watch stupid television with him." Me, too. Afterward, I wonder what could change this. What could a family member do that would make me sever my ties? I'm reminded of a recent conversation with my adolescent son and one of his friends. I had made some idle threat about what would happen if I caught them breaking some rule or law they seemed on the verge of flaunting. They pushed back and said, "Would you still love your children if they did drugs?" Of course. "What if they committed murder?" I don't know. "What if they grew up to be mean-spirited, money-grubbing assholes?" Sheesh. I suggested I might "love" but not "like" them. They rolled their eyes at this distinction, and we left it that they could go out, get stoned, get arrested, fight off the cops, grow up, become cops themselves—even mean, dirty cops like the ones that crushed Serpico or gratuitously beat Occupy protestors—and I would still love them. But as soon as they shut the door, I thought maybe that was wrong, that there might be an end even to family love. So, I'm hesitant to ask my brother questions whose answers might make me stop caring for him, stop loving him. I tell myself I'll ask him more about his work the next time we talk, or I'll write an e-mail. But I don't.

I take some comfort rereading Paul Virilio's prescient 1983 book, *Pure War*. There, Virilio writes,

> I am against military intelligence, I am not against men of war. . . .
> They are dominated, whether they know it or not, by the war machine.
> So my opposition to war is an opposition to the essence of war in tech-
> nology, in society, in the philosophy of technology, etc. . . . They are no
> more responsible for the apocalyptic nature of war than the civilians.
> The proof is that they are disappearing, too! They're disappearing in the
> technology and automation of the war machine.[33]

Even then, Virillio could say, "The computer already has the last word. If the use of weapons is no longer taught at the Military Academy, it's because the time for decision is now insufficient. . . . The progressive elimination (which is already quite advanced) of the proletariat in the industrial machine runs parallel with the elimination of individuals in the war-machine." Virilio also reminds us, "All of us are already civilian soldiers, without knowing it. And some of us know it. The great stroke of luck for the military class's terrorism is that no one recognizes it. People don't recognize the militarized part of their identity, of their consciousness." I start to think of myself as one of the military's most successful secret soldiers, an ideological sleeper, a day-to-day Manchurian candidate. And I find myself nodding along when Virilio says, "Today, the military knows all about civilians, but civilians know nothing about the military. For me, this is the worst possible situation. *That's* the Apolitics of the Worst. . . . We must get inside Pure War, we must cover ourselves with blood and tears. We mustn't turn away. *That* is political and civil virtue."[34]

Jag Sidewinder Lima Charlie   That's weird   Did you hear who that was?

Yeah at this point I wouldn't I personally wouldn't be comfortable shooting at these
people   No   Uh esp especially just on DGS's   If I couldn't tell with
my own eyeball that they had weapons   I wouldn't just go off of DGS's uh
Yeah   Assessment for this reason

That lady is carrying a kid huh?   Maybe   No   No   Uh yeah
The baby I think on the right   Yeah   Yeah   The middle
Yeah

                    Right there in the crosshairs

                                        explicative let them know dude

For a while, I take a break from puppets and become obsessed with emblems and devices. Like puppets, they simplify, stand in for, condense, and amuse. For a while, when I troll through reproductions of Renaissance emblems, they all remind me of drone politics. *Le Coeur du Roy est en le main de Dieu,* trumpets one where an engraved hand holding a huge crowned heart emerges from a bank of fluffy vellum clouds; this symbol of the church-backed state hovers menacingly over a village so tiny it is tender. In another, a porcupine, again wearing the king's crown of power, explodes with daggered quills; it is accompanied by the inscription *Cominus et Eminus* ("From near and afar") referring to the belief that porcupines could shoot their quills at their enemies from a distance. And then there is the image of a smiling anthropomorphic cloud beaming its rays onto a heart hunkered down on the ground. The inscription reads, "The mind should have a fixed eye on objects that are placed on high." While I am writing about these images, the *New York Times* runs an op-ed accompanied by a woodcut of a drone, as seen from below, that has sprouted a large pair of angelic white wings.

Tableau. A gray papier mâché drone dangles from a string; it quivers above two young men posed beneath it, one hunched and cowering, one faceup, eyes raised and vulnerable. Their hands cover their ears to the whine. On the stage next to this scene is a second tableau. A cardboard commercial jet glides over a suburban swimming pool. Two women in big sunglasses lie faceup on chaise lounges; their hands, too, cover their ears. A banner festooned over the two scenes is emblazoned with the inscriptio: "The place where dreams meet." The silent scenes form the picture. Libretto translation screens mounted on the back of the seats flash the subscriptio: "The angel of death is on all sides." Oh oriflamme. What if this is the kind of essay you can make into a rubber stamp?

Icons, too, appeal. In the twelfth-century icon called "The Ladder of Divine Ascent" (named after the AD 600 ascetical treatise called the Κλίμαξ or *Scala* or *Climax Paradisi* and housed at St. Catherine's Monastery at the foot of Mount Sinai), a cluster of angels hover high up in a corner of the image. They watch as a group of lithe, silhouette devils attack a row of monks who are attempting to ascend a ladder to salvation. The devils are thin and black, wiry and agile. They carry ropes and long hooks with which they pull the ascending figures off the ladder. The devils maneuver easily through the golden air of the icon. Up in their corner, an audience of clustered angels make empty gestures of sorrow. They watch the devils do their jobs. (Contemporary allegories lie just beyond the frame.)

The *Scala* reminds me of "cloud ladders" used in sieges, the first of which was said to be built in 5th century BC China by Lu Ban, who also built one of the earliest autonomous mechanical birds. It was said that this unmanned aerial vehicle could hover for up to three days; one account said that it could take a man up in the air to spy on his enemies.[35]

I want to write with the simplicity and directness of the emblem and the icon, and, yes, perhaps with their didacticism, too. But more than that, I want to write a quiet essay like a black and white photo of the sea and the sky by Sugimoto. Monotone. Or even like his photos of natural history museum dioramas. Pictures of pictures of life. Not the teeming violence of actual death, but the strange stillness of the simulation. Quiet because dead but not dead. On the other hand, I don't want to oversimplify things. And there are so many things. Their accommodation seems to require not just the static constellation, but a poetics of multiplicity or of digression. "Poetics?" Edouard Glissant asks, and answers himself, "Precisely this double thrust, being a theory that tries to conclude, and a presence that concludes (presumes) nothing. Never one without the other. That is how the instant and duration comfort us. Every poetics is a palliative for eternity."[36]

Glissant's poetics of relation aims to inhabit both aesthetics and politics; it aims to be a "transformative mode of history." Can a poetics of

digression be similarly transformative? It hints at the prescriptive, realizes its own shortcomings, and veers away. It breaks into manifesto, and
then reconsiders. But always it moves toward its goal because a poetics
of digression is not the same as a poetics of wandering, or a poetics of
the incomplete, or the lost, or the chaotic, or the amorphous, the void,
or even, really, the fragment. The digression might leave its topic gently or abruptly, it might make a cut we can see or feel and thus create
a fragment, but it always wanders back, or on. A digression can only
be taken *from* a path, a direction, a destination—the terminus of argu-
ment or topic. In the most digressive of texts, the lines of exploration
might multiply into the connecting vectors of a constellation. But for
the most part, it is the possibility of tracing a central line that makes the
deviance of digression work. Think of Sterne's diagrams to Chapter 40
of *Tristram Shandy* where he charts his progress through volumes one
through four with four corresponding lines drawn left to right upon the
page, all riddled with cartoonish loops, potholes, cul-de-sacs, tumors,
and fissures charting his departures. On the next page, Sterne draws the
relatively smooth line of the fifth volume, about which he brags, he had
not taken "the least trifle" of a digression beyond a few "mere parenthe-
ses" (which appear as minor bumps and grooves in the track) until the
right-hand margin where, he recounts, some "devils led him the round
you see marked D." Figure D swoops out like a vast and lazy oxbow
before returning to the story.

The detour of digression might reveal or illuminate something significant about the central exploration, or the deviance might simply give us
a break, a relief from direction, the pleasure of undirected leisure, the
chance to step away from the work. This is the politics of the poetics of
digression. To claim that the pleasures of the undirected ramble is the
politics of a poetics of digression recognizes that to wander, to roam,
are leisure activities. A stroll is a way of spending one's time, of taking
one's time, away from work. In his first walk of his *Reveries of a Solitary
Walker*, Rousseau says that he is "incapable" of proceeding with "method
and order" and that "it would even take away from" his goal of becoming aware of his "soul and its sequence." So he resolves to be "content to
keep a record of the measurements without seeking to reduce them to a

system." He compares his enterprise to that of Montaigne who describes his approach as having "rhetorical arrangements which are free and undisciplined" and of being a "formless way of speaking, free from rules and in the popular idiom, proceeding without definitions, subdivisions and conclusions."[37] Montaigne reminds us that it is "a thorny undertaking . . . to follow a movement so wandering as that of our mind."[38]

It is time for a walk. We take a narrow prairie trail by the muddy brown river. My companion is quoting Stevens: "All night I sat reading a book / Sat reading as if in a book." It is a sweet delirium to leave the rutted path of our jobs for this late afternoon reverie of transport as a dark cloud of starlings explodes above us and the light turns the grassy bank yellow. Sweet to stop walking and lie on the muddy verge of the swollen river under the spell of the gyrating black cloud of birds busy with compression and expansion. Like a poem. I want to be reincarnated as that murmuration, that concatenation of singularities. A starling consciousness where each bird is one, autonomous, but also able to work intuitively with others, to be an element of an aggregate mind effortlessly engaged in collective behavior. Each starling controls itself and is also controlled by the others, all pulling each others' strings like some giant, soaring, undulating puppet.

"There are many forms of the swarm, but the most often cited in military strategy are those of the ant and bee. For example, John Arquilla—an early proponent of swarming in the Department of Defense (DOD) analysis, an adviser to many generals, and a chief military adviser to Rumsfeld—wrote in his famous RAND Corporation study, *Swarming and the Future of Conflict,* that swarming needs to replace the AirLand Battle doctrine that has been the conceptual framework for the U.S. Army's European war fighting policy from 1982 up to the shock and awe techniques of the Iraq War. AirLand Battle emphasized close coordination between aggressively maneuvering land forces and air forces attacking frontline enemy forces. Swarming, as Arquilla and others define it, decentralizes

force operations in a way that values mobility, unit autonomy, and
continuous and synchronized real-time communication. Swarming
entails the 'systematic pulsing of force or fire by dispersed, inter-
knitted units, so as to strike the adversary from all directions simultaneously' (Arquilla and Ronseldt 2002:23)."

—Jake Kosek: "Ecologies of Empire:
On the New Uses of the Honeybee"[39]

When I tell my friends about my longing for starling consciousness,
someone always brings up Michael Hardt and Antonio Negri's *Multitude,* in which the authors sketch out a radical new form of politics
based on the swarm, whose members "do not have to become the same
or renounce their creativity in order to communicate and cooperate
with each other."[40] It is a notion Franco Berardi challenges, saying that
in the digital age, while we do tend to function as a swarm, this swarm
is of an automatic nature, reminding me again of the puppet with its
knee-jerk responses, its inability to truly gain autonomy. Berardi says
the swarm cannot be political because the information we must process
is "too much: too fast, too intense, too thick and complex for individuals or groups to elaborate it consciously, critically, reasonably, with the
necessary time to make a decision."[41]

Yeah they called out the kid   Yep I got another kid

That's one of the adolescents from earlier   That's good for Bam Bam   Yeah
sure is   Bam Bam41 Kirk97 uh just be advised uh our DGS is calling out uh
potential 3 females and uh 2 adolescents uh near the center vehicle   uh just want
to confirm that you saw that and passed to Jag Bam Bam41   Roger

Uh not sure on the adolescents   uh did a uh low pass and have uh 3
individuals in a brighter dress garb supposedly females

You got one carrying a child   They called it out   And that's affirm from Kirk97

It looks like uh one of those in the uh bright garb may be carrying a child as well
Uh be advised uh DGS is calling that at this time uh they did not call it prior to
this   *radio static*   Younger than a adolescent to me   Well   But
that's   that's   I mean   No way to tell   man   No way to tell from here
That's a kid there   to the left   Yeah that's what they were calling the
adolescent earlier

                                        Yeah adolescents don't move like that

```
Articulation means connection. /
            A jointed location that permits movement.
            / A linked structure or series. / The separation of successive notes, one
            from
another. / The utterance
                    of distinct elements of speech. /
                            The expression, in words, of something
                            immaterial or abstract such as an emotion or idea. /
                                    / Clarity, distinctness (now rare).
```

Some puppets are articulated and so are some essays. Some thoughts are harder to articulate than others.

The poetics of digression may simply be the poetics of the essay. As Adorno says in "The Essay as Form," the essay always "abandons the main road to the origin." It accentuates "the fragmentary, the partial rather than the total," it "does not strive for closed, deductive, or inductive, construction." Adorno tells us that "Discontinuity is essential to the essay; its concern is always conflict brought to a standstill."[42] The conflict brought to a standstill is part of the politics of a poetics of digression. The unexpected turn in our path offers an oblique or transitory glimpse of the thoroughfare of our lives and its struggles. For Adorno, one of those struggles is the incessant tyranny of work. He writes, "The essay mirrors what is loved and hated instead of presenting the intellect on the model of a boundless work ethic." The essay takes a break even as it resists. Or so we might insist. Utopias are the hidden territories of most poetics. "The surrealist idea of drifting or aimless wandering is a prime example," Michael Löwy writes, of "a protest against narrow-minded rationality, the commercialization of life." Surrealism's poetics of digression is, as Löwy writes, an "eminently subversive attempt to re-enchant the world," whose desire for escape was never escapist, but revolutionary—always directed to a liberation both magical and materialist.[43]

"Thesis I. There was once, we know, an automaton constructed in such a way that it could respond to every move by a chess player with a countermove that would ensure the winning of the game. A puppet wearing Turkish attire and with a hookah in its mouth sat before a chessboard placed on a large table. A system of mirrors created the illusion that this table was transparent on all sides. Actually, a hunchback dwarf—a master at chess—sat inside and guided the puppet's hand by means of strings.[44] One can imagine a philosophic counterpart to this apparatus. The puppet, called 'historical materialism' is to win all the time. It can easily be a match for anyone if it enlists the services of theology, which today, as we know, is small and ugly and has to keep out of sight."

—Walter Benjamin, *Theses on the Concept of History*, 1940

How strange to find historical materialism as the puppet—the awkward sad-faced pawn and not the sovereign string-puller. The manipulated contraption, not the controlling force behind the scenes or even the scenery itself. How disorienting to see historical materialism, that "vision of history as a permanent struggle between the oppressed and the oppressors"[45] looking both mysterious and comic in a fur-trimmed robe, a turban, and a wilted mustache. His pantograph-controlled gestures both mesmerizing and precise. And yet, the analogic figure has a winking appeal. With its rolling gray eyes, its brass cabinet full of clicking clockwork machinery (a whirring ruse of gleaming geometries), and its incredible skill at chess (it was only occasionally beaten by the rare chess master), the Turk was a curiosity precisely because it seemed to be at once a puppet, and not one. At once something operated by humans, and an autonomous system with its own internal logic. The puppet was promoted as "The Mechanical Turk" and was described as an independent machine, an automaton, an artificial intelligence. In fact, it helped inspire Charles Babbage, who lost a game to the Turk in 1819, to invent his Difference and Analytical Engines, which we now know to have spawned the true match for 20th-century historical materialism; the information network's post-Fordist victory over both the machine and the labor politics it birthed now nearly complete. But from the Mechanical Turk's first appearance, it was hard for people to believe that his skill, particularly his flexibility in responding to a range of opponents, was possible without a hidden humanity. As a 1784 pamphlet had speculated, "Whatever his outward form be composed of, he bears a living soul within."[46] The revelation of its secret power was that this was so: the Turk was not an unconscious, mechanical, autonomous system, but, rather, a puppet.

In Benjamin's analogy, the revelation of historical materialism was that it, too, was not autonomous, or rather that it should not be; that it must have at its core a revivifying soul of a theology reliant on remembrance and redemption. Michael Löwy tells us that for Benjamin, the Fascist victories over the Marxist labor movement in Western Europe demonstrated "the incapability of this soulless puppet, this insensate automaton [historical materialism], to 'win the game'—a game in which the future of humanity is at stake." For Benjamin, the martyrs of past struggles, according to Löwy, "await from us not just the remembrance of their suffering, but reparation for past injustices and the achievement of their social utopia."[47] This is what leads to redemption—a messianic power born of individuals and collective actions. The live person, cramped and vital within the machine, within the puppet, must use remembrance and reparation as ways to struggle effectively.

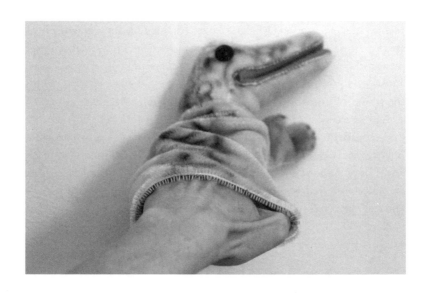

What animates a puppet? A body and soul bent on representing affect through gesture? What animates a human? Franco Berardi says mind, language, and creativity, and he calls that the "soul." He calls that the soul and suggests that it is the primary tool for the production of value under semiocapitalism. "Putting the soul to work," he writes, "is the new form of alienation." But alienation is not just something negative; experiencing an "estrangement from capitalistic interest" is a "necessary condition for the construction—in a space estranged from and hostile to labor relations—of an ultimately human relationship."[48] What animates us is exploited, and this recognition offers us the possibility of resisting that exploitation by redeploying the mind, language, and creativity.

Politically, what kind of reanimation do we need? Are we anesthetized by our existence, or already overly animated—zoned out online or too busy running the program of our own Chaplinesque modern times to do anything other than keep pace with the system? The question of the relationship of animation to political will and autonomy has been raised many times before. In his work on Keats and Shelley, Robert Mitchell traces two different responses to questions of animation and agency in Romanticism, saying writers following Coleridge's lead "saw suspended animation as a dangerous condition, and they employed the concept to describe a loss of subjective autonomy produced by the distractions of modernity," while Keats and Shelley saw suspended animation "as a potentially desirable state that could regulate the otherwise swift and automatic animations of modern life." Mitchell writes, "Where Coleridge feared suspended animation, seeing in it only a narcosis of the will, Keats and the Shelleys aimed at a poetics of trance, deploying literary form as a technology that could vitalize readers' will and understanding by suspending animation." Mitchell adds,

> Keats and Shelley's practice . . . suggests that a politically engaged aesthetics must do more than awaken a population frozen in automaticity; it must also seek to produce suspensions in those who are already too animated. Suspension, in this sense, empowers their differential capacities of sensation, which in turn makes possible new forms and objects of willing.[49]

Puppets' peculiar animation—an animation that is not truly their own, that does not resemble individual will, that relies on others, but is nonetheless powerful, is one such form of willing, one that might reanimate my threadbare sense of possible actions.

Theories plunder like rain. The ground washes away in muddy snakes. Just when you get a glimpse, the pounding sound of water courses through the metal gutters. We're trying to make sense of white noise, but it's just rain. Videos the size of quarters. Croyden's burning. Cairo's rising. Oakland's stirring. A cluster is a kettle. Yemen is no image. Ferguson is everywhere and time opens something that feels like a thought. The operator holds from behind. Black clothes. Black hood. You can feel him pushing. We're surging forward now, right to the undulating waves at the edge of the stage. What are you hoping for? Flowers bursting in fractal ecstasy? The roar of the crowd? What do you think this is? The end of the world? The beginning?

When is a puppet like a robot? A joke in search of a punch line. In the Marx reading group, almost every meeting devolves into the question of a robot future. The utopia capitalism can't allow because it does away with the possibility of surplus value. Viva la robot. Except when language is the robot. When the silvery time-saver speaks me. Then fight the robot and love the robot. (The word *robot* first appeared in a Czech story in 1920 and is derived from the Slavic word for "hard work," "labor," or "drudgery"; the story, *Rossum's Universal Robots,* explored the exploitation of artificial humans.) Convert the robot. Make the robot run my insurrection. Automata, too, are inanimate subjects.

In 1718, at Waltham Abby in England, Henry Bridges constructed a large tabletop automaton called "The Microcosm." When it was exhibited in 1756 in Philadelphia, *The New York Mercury* listed the elements of this "world in miniature": "1. All the celestial phenomena are shown.

2. The nine Muses, giving a concert. 3. Orpheus in the forest. 4. A carpenter's shop. 5. A delightful grove. 6. A beautiful landscape with a distant view of the sea. 7. Lastly, all the machinery of the piece, including 1,200 wheels and pinions in motion."[50] There is something so tender about this clockwork world with its clashes of the pastoral and machinic. The quiet grove, the distant sea, and the whirring, shifting, clicking riot of the new. What would a contemporary "world in miniature" be? A curiosity of nanotechnology that can be seen only under a microscope? Maybe it could show: 1. The complete human genome. 2. The G-7 giving an edict. 3. A tiny terrorist in a bedroom. 4. A microdrone hovering at the window. But we could never achieve the same startling juxtaposition of the natural world with the technological one that Bridges' mechanical "Microcosm" offered. This jolt is only available to us now in moments of disaster. The streaming video of brown oil gushing from BP's submerged pipe. Helicopters scooping water from the sea to dump on Japan's melting nuclear reactor. The latest earthquake-tumbled shantytown. The floodwaters swamping the metropolis. All miniaturized on screen. What might charm us today is the world in macrocosm. A reversal of scale. The exhilaration of feeling ourselves miniaturized, freed from any sense of bored over-familiarity with, or responsibility for, the cosmos. A giant robotic baby squeezing the gushing oil spill closed between its chubby thumb and finger. A battalion of hot-air balloon firemen floating with their hoses over the burning reactor. A colossal hand casually crushing the unmanned aerial vehicle.

Well don't forget the women and children dude   I know I know   OK
It's got to go through a lot of shit if he expects to shoot

                              Arrow30 copies all and uh we do see three vehicles
first and third being destroyed the second one looks like a blue uh SUV similar to a
Bronco with a white top   That's a good copy uh we are contact at you are
eyes on our location at that time   Uh be advised uh about 20 meters to the
west of that uh Potential Bronco uh there's what our DGS uh is calling as three
women and two children

                    Uh but you are on the right area   Arrow is our manned ISR?
Yep   Yeah   Arrow three zero copies   Three women and children just
to 20 meters to the west of this second vehicle And that is affirm for Kirk97
Since the engagement we have not been able to PID any weapons three-zero.

Dude I don't know 'cause we watched these guys stop multiple times and every time
they were all wearin all black and only afterwards did we ever see any color It's
possible the women and children never got out of the car at the stops

                                                                          Yeah

                    [Unintelligible statement]

Jag25   Kirk97   Jag25   Kirk97   Jag25   Jag25
Kirk97   Kirk97   Jag25   Jag25   Kirk97   [Static]
mic check   Uh Jag28 may be outside of the wire at this time and uh

                                        moving on his own mission

                    [end of transcription]

                              ⌖

"On Feb. 21, 2010, a convoy of vehicles carrying civilians headed
down a mountain in central Afghanistan. American eyes were
watching. For more than four hours, the U.S. military—including a Predator drone crew in Nevada, video screeners in Florida,
an AC-130 airplane crew in the sky and an American special operations unit on the ground nearby—tracked the convoy, trying to
decide whether it was friend or foe. This is the official U.S. military transcript of the radio transmissions and cockpit conversations
that day, obtained by the Los Angeles Times through a Freedom of
Information Act request."

> —David S. Cloud, "Transcripts of
> U.S. drone attack," *Los Angeles Times*[51]

I worked with this transcript as my source document. I removed some
sections and some words, but I kept close to the original sequence and
tried to stay faithful to what I found to be the central elements of the
transcript—the events, the broken communications, the people on both
sides of the screen, as much as they are made visible here. And then I
looked for something from the other side.

The following are excerpts from a transcript of a conversation between
members of the CodePink Peace Delegation to Pakistan and Karim
Khan, a man from a village near Mir Ali, Pakistan, whose teenage
son, his younger brother, and a guest were killed by a drone attack on
his home while he was away at work. Posted on November 6, 2012,
by Upstate Drone Action. Recorded and transcribed by Leah Bolger of
Voices for Peace.

The tribal people, we are facing very difficult problems, first of all I
would like to say we are members of a tribal territory of the sovereign
state which name is Pakistan. It is not a part of Afghanistan. We are
the tribal people of Pakistan. So they started to attack our tribal people
by drone airplanes. I think that the American people are telling a lie to
everyone and everywhere. In these drone attacks they attack my house

also. It was 31st December 2009 and they said that we killed a number
of AQ [Al Qaida] terrorists, but in fact in this drone attack there were
only three persons. One was my beloved son, named Zaheenullah, and
the other was my younger brother named Asid Iqbal, and the third one
was a mason by profession, he was constructing a mosque for us in
that village. . . . They killed these persons and they said that they killed
"Adjuma." I told these people yesterday that after some months, they
announced in another drone attack, they announced that once again
they killed the same person, named Adjuma. And after some months
in another drone attack, they announced once again that they killed
Adjuma. We are astonished and we are wondering whether a man has
one death or several deaths; a man has one life or several lives. And
so they said that we have killed a commander named Ilias Kashmiri.
I think he is alive until now. And after this they said in another drone
strike, we killed Ilias Kashmiri and after some months, once again they
announced once again that we killed Kashmiri in another drone strike.
And after several times they announced this. But I think he is alive
until now. But the people who were killed in these drone attacks. Who
were they?

They are announcing and telling people that we are killing AQ terrorists,
Taliban terrorists. But in fact they are not AQ people, they are not AQ
members, they are not Taliban member. They are ordinary people. And
they are killing ordinary people. So they are killing our Muslim people,
our innocent people, our tribal people, and they are living in Pakistan.
They are not in Afghanistan. There is a battle there, there are difficulties,
there are problems between them—the whole world and the Taliban
in Afghanistan, not in Pakistan. Pakistan is our territory—a peaceful
territory in the whole world. It's calm; it's peaceful. And the American
people only want to disturb this territory to disturb peace and stability
in territory. When they want to attack any house, they attack it. No one
stops them, no one say any word, no one raises their voice against this,
that they are killing innocent people. So they are only blaming us, they
are telling a lie to you people that we are killing AQ, terrorists, Taliban
terrorists, but in fact, it's not true. It's my house. So if there is any
terrorist, any person present here in this assembled people, if someone

wants to kill him, then he will kill ALL these people? And America and
other NATO forces and the whole world they could arrest them. For
example, if there is any person, he's a criminal, and he has done something wrong, they can arrest him. And they can bring him to court. But
it's not a good manner of killing, to kill several people for one man.
You see my house. It's completely destroyed. You see my beloved son,
my brother. This is my son. He memorized the Quran. He was 16 years
old. They took my house and killed him, and they say that we killed
"Adjuma." Here is Adjuma? This is my beloved son, Zaheenullah. And
in another, there is my brother, Asif Iqbal. Here is my brother and here
is my son. I have their service books. They have a book from government of Pakistan. Maybe you people also have service books?

That is only one case. You will see in every case, we have a lot of pictures
of these people. Images of houses and killed people and injured people.
They are smart. They are kids, they are innocent people killed by these
drone strikes. Ah, there is another person. He was in Jirga. A meeting.
There was some problem between the people in the area, and they were
solving this problem. They assembled in a place, and then American
drone strike the place of the assembled people and killed these people.
And they said we killed terrorists. They are ordinary people. They are
not terrorists. More than 40 people were assembled in this area and
they were killed. And the place where these drone strikes are, I sent
my cousin to have a picture to have a record of this place. This was
same area—same. But the fire, the smoke, it was . . . after one week I
saw it in this area. It doesn't exist for more time, but after one week,
I saw this. That it is rising from the center. They are not only killing us—they are burning us. . . . They are not allowing us to go there
[to the U.S. Embassy] and to talk with them. They don't, I think they
don't consider us as a human being. Because it is inhuman this manner
that they are doing. If a human, he has a heart of flesh—he will never
do just like this. He will say, we have sons, we have brothers, we have
mothers and fathers, and if we are sitting in a house and someone attack
our house and kill our brother our mother, and everything will be
destroyed . . . what will be my reaction?[52]

At first, this book ended in despair.

But I made myself rewrite it.

Because we are, after all, still alive.

Like it or not.

"Bloch urges us to grasp the three dimensions of human temporality: he offers us a dialectical analysis of the past which illumi-
nates the present and can direct us to a better future. The past—
what has been—contains both the sufferings, tragedies and failures
of humanity—what to avoid and to redeem—and its unrealized
hopes and potentials—which could have been and can yet be. For
Bloch, history is a repository of possibilities that are living options
for future action, therefore what could have been can still be. . . .
Above all, Bloch develops a philosophy of hope and the future,
a dreaming forward, a projection of a vision of a future kingdom of
freedom. It is his conviction that only when we project our future
in the light of what is, what has been, and what could be can we
engage in the creative practice that will produce a world in which
we are at home and realize humanity's deepest dreams."
                                    —Douglas Kellner, "Ernst Bloch, Utopia,
                                              and Ideology Critique"[53]

Ladies figure skating comes on and my brother says, "Ladies? Really?
Women for everything else, but figure skating is *ladies?*" I have finally
gone to visit my brother. He has just retired from the Air Force. I am
happy to see him, happy to see our children together. The drug of family is working. On the last night of my stay, we're hanging out on the
couch having a glass of wine and watching the Olympics while our kids
ride their bikes around the neighborhood. It is a good day; I hate to
ruin it. But I am still thinking about drones and still thinking maybe
he can tell me something others can't. I don't think family relations are
privileged ones, the only ones that can bring me closer to some truth

about my world, but *not* asking him about his work with drones feels
like a weight I am carrying, a refusal to encounter anything that will
spill the pleasures of my privileged life. So, finally, I ask my brother if I
can interview him for my book; I tell him that he might not like what I
ask and how I use it. I tell him I won't misquote him and I'll try my best
not to misrepresent him, but I will use it in my own way. He shrugs
and says, yeah, actually he'd been hoping I'd ask and he'd like to do it.
I don't question him as relentlessly as an experienced journalist might,
but I ask what I can.

C: If drones are just another
weapon, do you think that the
publicity they receive forces people to confront the violence and
atrocities of war and that this is
what they really object to when
they object to drones?

C: Yes. But are we talking about
the impact of drones on war or
about American politics? If you
don't agree that we should be
attacking terrorists where they
are, that is a different issue and
one you could argue, but that is
not really about drones. The types
of things we are using to go after
them is immaterial. We're going
to use all the technology at our
disposal once we have decided to
go after them.

C: What do *you* think about
attacking terrorists where they
are?

C: I do think we should be
attacking them where they are,
but we have done it the wrong

way. We've put the money in the wrong places. I don't believe in nation building. I don't think we should be doing that. I don't think we should've put troops on the ground. I do think we should have gone after the terrorist camps with UAVs and Special Ops. We should have picked a few spots without putting our efforts into nation building. Going after terrorists to disrupt their operations is the right thing to do, but I see that as unrelated to drones.

C: What about the reports of drones killing members of wedding parties and civilians?

C: It has happened with other weapons. Apart from drones. It is reported. Maybe people just don't really care. Again, that doesn't have to do with drones, there've been plenty of civilian casualties with fighters and bombers. We've had that from . . . always. So it flabbergasts me that people think it is because of UAV technology. We've always done that. I don't deny that it is a little different, but in the end it is a platform that we created that delivers weapons. That is what the military does.

C: Is it naïve for citizens to object to the violence of war or necessary for them, for us, to do so?

C: This is the wrong question. War is violent and there will

always be war. It's a requirement
for civilians to object to unjust
military action. The violence
aspect is moot. War is violent.
Absolutely there are scenarios that
are unjust. It's a matter of opin-
ion if any of the recent scenarios
are unjust. I might say they were
horribly executed.

C: Is this war in Afghanistan
necessary?

C: I think we should leave imme-
diately. I think we've blown it.
I think way back in 2001 we
should have gone after terrorist
camps. I'm not a peace activ-
ist when it comes to that kind
of stuff, but instead we saw it
as a chance to put troops on
the ground and build back the
nation. But it doesn't work.
It didn't work in Vietnam,
it didn't work in Iraq, and it is
not going to work in Afghanistan.

C: Have any of the conflicts
you've been involved in seemed
necessary or justifiable?

C: [Long pause.] Yes. I'd classify
Bosnia as one of those. There
were so many different factions,
we could have sat by and let it
happen, but it could have spread
quickly and so I think that was
the right decision.

C: How much can you see when
you operate the drones? Can you
see people's faces?

C: Not quite to that level.

C: Did you like your job?

C: I liked the part of actively sup-
porting our troops on the ground.
Whatever your political bent is,
those guys have a very difficult
job—deployed away from their
families a year at a time. It felt
good to be helping to make their
lives safer. What UAVs do has
saved many lives on the ground.

C: Yeah, but they also take lives.
How do you deal with the fact
that you are killing people?

C: Easy. You do what you do
for the greater good. Those guys
we are going after are planning
terrorist attacks or are going after
women and children in their countries. You do whatever it takes.

C: Does it take a toll on you
personally?

C: Not for me personally, but I
did a whole lot of watching and
not a whole lot of taking action.
I was involved in a squadron that
was doing reconnaissance. But it
didn't bother me that others did
it. That is job satisfaction. The
caveat is that I was never involved
in or part of some action that
caused civilian casualties. I think
for the people who are involved
in that, it would be very difficult
not to feel horrible about it.

C: What questions do you think
U.S. citizens should be asking
about drones and about the
military?

C: None. It is a hardware. They should be the same questions you are asking about every weapons systems we have. The questions should be about U.S. foreign policy, not about the kind of technology that we are using to implement that foreign policy.

C: Do you know any pacifists? People who think that no war is justifiable. Sometimes I feel as though I can't object to anything the military state does unless I have this as my base position, but I can think of times when violence seems justifiable. You know, the usual examples—someone hurting my children, Hitler, fighting fascism. So, I don't know, is pacifism viable? Are questions like this irrelevant or necessary?

C: I don't know. How long have people been protesting military action? That would be good to know. And has pacifism ever worked against war?

C: Well, anti-war protests have worked. But maybe those successes were based more on an opposition to a particular conflict rather than the validity of war itself. Do you hope people like me will object to unnecessary conflicts and effectively limit them so you can stay safe and go to lacrosse practice with your kids? Or do you think it is impossible to limit conflicts?

C: I think there will always be
wars because the world is full of
people who see things differently.
Religious or cultural differences,
or power and greed, we'll always
be dealing with that. But again,
I am confused by the question,
because it sounds like you've got
two things going on in whatever
you're writing: drones, this new
technology and its impact, *and*
"Should the U.S. be sending military troops to these countries?"
Maybe that is the angle for your
piece: "What are we really talking
about here? What has got people
upset?" That to me is fascinating.
What those who are up in arms
are really concerned about is
something else.

C: What?

C: The long arm of the
U.S. military.

I can't stop thinking about my brother saying, "War is violent and there will always be war. It's a requirement for civilians to object to unjust military action. The violence aspect is moot." I agree with him absolutely. And then, suddenly, I don't. Something shifts and my belief that violence is sometimes necessary seems at least arguable. Suddenly, accepting both my brother's position, that there will always be violence and war, while also accepting the utopian vision of pacifism, that this can be changed, feels like a contradiction that is necessary. It seems at least possible to imagine a world where war, like slavery, is not so easily accepted. Yes, I know, slavery persists and erupts, but it is no longer thought to be either necessary or inevitable and, suddenly, I can imagine this for war. Wildly utopian, yes, but I lunge at this thought. I want to say "Time to act as a militant pacifist" even though I can barely glimpse it. Course corrections will no doubt be necessary. Still, the work is to find meaningful arenas for this belief and its possible actions, no? No easy task. In fact, just beginning to consider how to seek out such arenas beyond the personal makes me bone tired. A heavy curtain falls in front of this thought, and I am once again paralyzed in my seat. Who can cheer me on?

Ridiculous painted cherubs part the curtain; they reveal painted meadows and a painted temple. The entire scene rises into the rafters, exposing a group of tiny paper puppets. "Not for pleasure alone," states the carefully lettered sign on the puppet theater's proscenium arch in the prologue of Bergman's *Fanny and Alexander*. The puppet theatre has other work. Pleasure and horror; instruction and inspiration. Fear, illumination, motivation. But first, a tiny pleasure. A row of small yellow flames. Candle footlights to illuminate childhood dramas. Or traumas. Acts and wounds. A boy's head fills the stage. For a moment, he is framed by the glowing fantasy world. The boy twirls one of the cardboard puppets in his hand and places it on the stage. He considers the scene he has made and withdraws. The camera angle changes, and from the other side we see another head descend, the boy transformed into an old man. We have entered Bergman's *The Making of Fanny and*

Alexander. Through the opening of the miniature puppet theater, the director's face peers at us and at the boy he was. He is bringing something dead to life; he is animating the inanimate. Luminous in the radiance of the burning wax, Bergman says, "That, you see, is the greatest magic. It'll make your flesh crawl."

And it does. *Fanny and Alexander* lets me see something new about puppets. The film pulses with animism—the belief that all things, even inanimate ones, posses something like a spiritual essence, a consciousness—and it pulses, too, with the "omnipotence of thought" wherein thinking itself gains agency. Objects in the film possess awareness, ideas take action, souls are disembodied or mingled. A white marble statue beckons Alexander to her naked breast. ("A secret terror from my childhood," Bergman confides.) The crystals in the chandelier clink in no breeze. A doll raises her arms and turns her head. In a bedtime story, a humble wooden chair radiates a mysterious light, glows from within, bringing with it a kind of transcendence. ("Look how it shines!") Figures of the children, wax models or enchantments, lie asleep on their prison floor while the real children are spirited away in a trunk to Uncle Isak's puppet shop home with its wooden kings and demons, its disembodied heads and limbs. There, a giant God puppet falls, grinning, and a white-faced Japanese puppet twitches its clearly human hand. A mummy breathes visibly. ("Uncle Isak says that we're surrounded by different realities, one on top of the other. There are swarms of ghosts, spirits, phantoms, souls, poltergeists, angels, and demons. He says the smallest pebble has a life of its own.") The examples pile up. They never really frighten, and are, in fact, a comfort and a deliverance from the daily terror of a real, malevolent, and punitive authority.

"Perhaps we're the same person with no boundaries," Ismael, the mad cousin in *Fanny and Alexander,* suggests. "Perhaps we flow through each other, stream through each other boundlessly and magnificently," and, standing behind Alexander, manipulates his body as if it were a puppet. Alexander, in turn, imagines a distant hand toppling a lamp, and it

does. He wills his oppressors to burn, and they do. His thoughts are a
puppet gone wild.

Just as the puppet Hari offered *Solaris'* Kris a more consequential love
than the human Hari, Bergman's puppets provide a curious assemblage
of solace and agency that is at once imaginary and real. Isn't the mysti-
cism of the interconnection of souls, bodies, and objects a more prom-
ising credo than a rational, monadic impotence? Isn't the limited autonomy of a puppeted self better than the despairing powerlessness of a
humanist self whose agency might be illusory?

Time has passed, my children are on the cusp of adulthood. I am in
Paris with my younger son; he is taller than me and crushes me with
his hugs. We are walking in the Jardins du Luxembourg on a day like a
painting. The sky is all steel gray and dark inky blue, like a burden and
a joy, like privilege. The sun glares in our eyes and rain falls behind us.
We walk past the children's playground with its stiff green metal swings,
giant cradles swooping crazily high and fast. There can never be enough
days like this one. There is a small building in front of us. My son stops
abruptly and grabs my arm. "Mom, Mom, it's the puppet theater from
The 400 Blows!" And it is. Les Marionnettes du Luxembourg founded
in 1933 by Robert Desarthis. The sign says today's show is *Pinocchio*.
It begins at 3:15. I ask my son what time it is, he takes out his phone,
pulls a face, and turns the phone to face me. It is 3:15. He smiles broadly,
and we move forward to buy our tickets from the founder's son, Francis-
Claude, who now runs the theatre. He is a short, squat, balding man
with heavy, smudged, theatrical eye makeup. He is precisely the counter-
agent to conformity you didn't know you needed. What I mean is, his
eccentricity is deeply comforting; his strangeness makes him a friend.

We step into the theatre, nearly as giddy with excitement as the dozens
of tiny children filling the long low wooden benches in front of the little

stage. The walls are painted in three broad horizontal stripes: pumpkin, ox-blood, green-room green. It's pretty great. Posters of the puppet stars circle the room: Le Chat Botte, Le Duc, Pinnochio, and Guignol, the puppet Master of Ceremonies in his traditional black cap and long black pigtail of the 18th-century Lyonnaise silk-weaver he once was. The lights go out, and in the flat black, the children are suddenly quiet. The silence makes the blackness weirdly dense until the curtain rises on a wildly vivid teal green and scarlet living room. Guignol enters and speaks directly to the children, luring them into the story of Pinocchio, who emerges from behind the cover of the book Guignol has begun to read, but which he has put down for a moment to look out the window behind him. The children *ooh* in unison and then yell, "Guignol! Guignol! Look! Pinocchio! Behind you! Turn around! Guignol!" The room is a box of squealing noise. I look at my son and at the row of adults sitting along the edge of the theatre on folding chairs; even in the dim blue-black light, I can see that they are smiling and rising up in their seats. The children's vitality wakes us up.

As the play unfolds, Pinocchio is told by the Blue Fairy that he must go on an adventure where he will learn to stop lying, learn to be brave, and, in an odd but predictable twist, learn his ABC's. In the end, after a wild journey through a lurid ochre and violet landscape filled with wild lions, evil men, and talking frogs, it is Pinocchio's ability to recite the alphabet that truly impresses the Blue Fairy and leads her to grant his wish to be turned into a real boy. She twirls her "baguette magique" and the wooden puppet Pinocchio with his goggly eyes and obviously jointed legs is transformed into—wait for it—yet another puppet. The transformed Pinocchio looks like an oversized baby doll with soft, rounded, cherubic features. The change is magical, but, well, he is clearly not a real boy. (I half expected a live child actor to appear at that moment.) Guignol says to him, "There, now you are a real boy!" and Pinocchio replies, "No! Really? Am I truly a real boy?" Guignol says, "Ask the children." Pinocchio turns to face the rows of children and asks them, "Is it true? Am I now a real boy?" There is a slight hesitation as they are faced with a difficult choice: either they can accept the lesson of the play and tell the truth ("No. No, Pinocchio, you are still a puppet")

and hurt Pinocchio's feelings (which are palpable even if not real) and ruin the moment, or they can ignore everything they've been taught and follow what is clearly an exhortation, here and now, to lie.

'They lie. "Yes!" they yell. "Yes! You're a real boy!"

On the one hand, the audience has clearly been manipulated into telling this comforting lie. The difficulty of telling the truth, of opposing the official story, has been made impossible by the pressure to maintain the joy of the moment. But on the other hand, the lie is only told out of love. The children aren't lying to cover their own misdeeds; they are not betraying Pinocchio. They only want him to know that he is real to them, or at least, real enough. His incomplete transformation is sufficient. They want to spare him from suffering, a suffering they know he feels even as they know him to be an object. They want to tell him the possibility for change he so longs for is still real.

There is no one way to be real. We all grow up to be puppets, there is nothing outside of the manipulations we live within, but we are real enough, we can act on our little stage.

The closing lines of Bergman's film are from Strindberg's *A Dream Play*: "Everything can happen. Everything is possible and probable. Time and space do not exist. On a flimsy framework of reality, the imagination spins, weaving new patterns." Perhaps we, too, flow through each, stream through each other boundlessly and magnificently. Everything is possible and probable.

"Even as the defeated are lying there, they're already confronted
with larger as yet unfought battles and the likelihood of self-
produced disaster, they must now be addressed with the Possibilitarian imperative to rise up to their past battle history existence . . .
the anti-disaster battle cry, the battle cry that life demands of them
to realize the Possibilitarian word, the possible world that the disaster world needs."

—Peter Schumann, Bread and Puppet Theater

"'History' and its politics are not the only theme of the historical
imaginary; it centrally involves thoughts and fantasies about the
subject itself, about its position in the symbolic order, about its
desires and anxieties, about life and death, and about love. The historical imaginary is the way in which we live the symbolic order as
historical; its nature determines whether we are enabled and enable
ourselves to act as historical-political subjects—or whether we fail
to do so. *History as catastrophe* positions us as subjected to an order
over which we have no control."

—Julia Hell, "Remnants of Totalitarianism: Hannah Arendt,
Heiner Müller, Slavoj Žižek, and the Re-Invention of Politics"[54]

I am still trying to show you something. Ardent. Chromatic. The only
visual analogy I can find for this yearning is one of those 3-D Imax mov-
ies of the universe where you zoom through the Hubble Space Telescope
images with everything expanding infinitely all around you. Everything
is in motion. Everything is limitless. It is the deepest pleasure. You pass
through one gorgeous nebula, then another, and then we're zooming
out to show that this seeming infinity was only one small speck in one
tiny region. Look around, it is infinite, with its tufted chartreuse and
indigo pillars, its soft columns of cool interstellar hydrogen gas and
dust. Now, we're moving backward and twirling, and another part of
space expands vertiginously, magenta and black, endlessly opening onto
something immense and new.

"Getting your puppet off the stage is just as important as getting it
on. Time your exits so that there is no awkward pause between the
last word spoken and the exit."
                              —Winifred H. Mills and Louise M. Dunn.
                              Marionettes, Masks, and Shadows. 1931[55]

Maybe now it is time to put away the plaything of this puppet figure
in favor of a more active one, something that reminds us of the ways in
which we are not puppets and that drones are not our masters, but we
theirs. Maybe I'll cut the strings and turn all these puppets into effigies.
Effigies are puppets that burn. Effigies are politics in action. Effigies
don't have a puppet's spirited animation, but their makers do. When the
flames engulf the effigy, we don't see the doll, only the daring.

ACKNOWLEDGMENTS

Over the years, many people helped me with this book. I am so grateful to all of them. A few who read drafts, published excerpts, or were supportive in other crucial ways were Leslie Brack, Mary Cappello, Teju Cole, Stephen Cope, Caroline Crumpacker, Rob Halpern, Joe Harrington, Naeem Inayatullah, Wayne Koestenbaum, Amitava Kumar, David Lazar, Patrick Madden, PJ Mark, Anna Moschovakis, Nicholas Muellner, Maggie Nelson, Jena Osman, Ed Pavlic, Wylie Schwartz, Jonathan Skinner, Chuck Taylor, Maxwell Taylor-Milner, Emrys Taylor-Milner, Brian Teare, David Weiss, Rebecca Wolff, Andrew Zawacki, Bread and Puppet Theater, The MacDowell Colony, Yaddo, The Millay Colony, and The Saltonstall Foundation. Special thanks to my editor, Kristen Elias Rowley.

NOTES

1 Debord, *The Society of the Spectacle,* 2.
2 Bumiller, "Airforce Drone Operators Report."
3 Plato, *The Laws,* 644e–645b.
4 Rivera, "Border Control."
5 King, "Beyond Vietnam," kingencyclopedia.stanford.edu.
6 Bumiller, "Air Force Drone Operators."
7 Ibid.
8 Sparrow, "Building a Better WarBot."
9 Graham, *Cities Under Siege,* 168.
10 Lal, "Micro and Nano."
11 Daryl Hauck quoted in Graham, *Cities Under Siege,* 173–74.
12 Graham, *Cities Under Siege,* 169.
13 Lawton, "The Ethics of Drones."
14 Barrett, "Rise of the Drones," 2.
15 Ibid.
16 The seventeenth-century radicals known as "The Diggers" dug and planted on common grounds as part of their fight against private ownership.
17 Wood, *Modernism in Dispute,* 15.
18 Rockwell, "Theater."
19 Dickson, "Ariane Mnouchkine."
20 Cixous, *Tambours Sur La Digue.*
21 Jenkins, "Theater; As if They Are Puppets."
22 Sorgenfrei, "Production Review."
23 For philosopher Georg Lukács, the conventional subject thinks of himself or herself as voluntary but is everywhere constrained. For Lukács, the only way we can begin to both understand our world and have the possibility to change it is through our understanding of ourselves as workers. This is because every time the worker "imagines himself to be the subject of his own life, he finds this to be an illusion that is destroyed by the immediacy of his existence." We see that we are products of the world of work; our own selves a kind of commodity. An object. A puppet. "But," Lukács writes, "because of the split between subjectivity and

objectivity induced in him by the compulsion to objectify himself as a commodity, the situation becomes one that can be made conscious." Thus, we can become conscious of what Marx calls the "social character of labour," and the normally abstract forces that limit us can be concretized, seen, understood, and, hence, overcome. Lukács, *History and Class Consciousness,* 165, 168.

[24] Karzai, "Karzai: Are You An American Puppet?"

[25] Favret, *War at a Distance,* 11.

[26] Batchelder, *The Puppet Theatre Handbook.*

[27] Rancière, *The Emancipated Spectator,* 2.

[28] Stewart-Steinberg, *The Pinocchio Effect,* 23–24.

[29] Boon, "The Eternal Drone."

[30] Shaw, "Note on Puppets."

[31] Kliest, "On the Marionette Theatre."

[32] Adorno, *Negative Dialectics,* 162–166.

[33] Virilio, *Pure War,* 33–34, 119–20, 179.

[34] Ibid.

[35] Di, "Lu Ban."

[36] Glissant, *Poetics of Relation,* 183.

[37] Montaigne, *Michel de Montaigne,* 724–25.

[38] Montaigne, *The Complete Essays of Montaigne,* 273.

[39] Kosek, "Ecologies of Empire."

[40] Hardt and Negri, *Multitude,* 91–92.

[41] Berardi, *The Soul at Work,* 194–95.

[42] Adorno, "The Essay As Form," 152, 157, 158, 159, 164.

[43] Löwy, *Fire Alarm,* 1.

[44] According to Mark Sussman, this is the automaton first presented in 1770 by its inventor, the Baron von Kempelen, to the Austrian Empress Maria Theresa. It was shown in London in 1783 along with "a Speaking Figure, a doll that faintly, though audibly answered questions posed to it," (Sussman, 77–78). It played many curious admirers and chess fiends, including Benjamin Franklin and Napoleon. After Von Kempelen died in 1804, it was bought by Johann Maelzel, who added a voice box that declared "échec!" whenever it was in check. In 1836, Edgar Allan Poe wrote an essay, later translated by Baudelaire, revealing some of its secrets. While the Turk machine did use a series of magnets and levers, Benjamin was right that there was a man inside the machine, but it was not a dwarf. A series of chess masters are known to have operated from within ("The Turk," Wikipedia).

[45] Löwy, *Fire Alarm,* 32.

[46] Sussman, "Performing the intelligent machine," 80.

[47] Löwy, *Fire Alarm,* 25, 32.

[48] Berardi, *The Soul at Work,* 23.

49 Mitchell, "Suspended Animation," 109, 119.

50 Sussman, "Performing the intelligent machine," 78.

51 Cloud, "Transcripts of U.S. drone attack."

52 Khan, *Transcript of the meeting with Karim Khan.*

53 Kellner, "Ernst Bloch, Utopia, and Ideology Critique," 81–82.

54 Hell, "Remnants of Totalitarianism."

55 Mills and Dunn, *Marionettes, Masks, and Shadows.*

BIBLIOGRAPHY

"A—Hybrid Insect MEMS (HI-MEMS)." *Federal Business Opportunities.* Last modified March 9, 2006. https://www.fbo.gov/index?s=opportunity&mode =form&id=ec6d6847537a9220810f4282eedda0d2&tab=core&_cview=1.

Adorno, Theodor W. "The Essay As Form." *New German Critique,* no. 32 (Spring–Summer 1984): 151–71.

———. *Negative Dialectics.* London: Bloomsbury Academic, 1981.

Anderson, Becky. "Karzai: Terrorists could regain control." *CNN.* Last modified January 26, 2008. http://www.cnn.com/2008/WORLD/europe/01/25 /karzai.interview/.

Barrett, Edward. "Rise of the Drones: Unmanned Systems and the Future of War." Statement to the House Committee on Oversight and Government Reform Subcommittee on National Security and Foreign Affairs. March 23, 2010. www.fas.org/irp/congress/2010_hr/032310barrett.pdf.

Batchelder, Marjorie. *The Puppet Theatre Handbook.* New York: Harper and Brothers, 1947.

Berardi, Franco "Bifo." *The Soul at Work: From Alienation to Autonomy.* Los Angeles, CA: Semiotext(e), 2009.

Boon, Marcus. "The Eternal Drone." Last modified March 9, 2003. http:// marcusboon.com/the-eternal-drone/.

Bumiller, Elisabeth. "Air Force Drone Operators Report High Levels of Stress." *The New York Times.* Last modified December 18, 2011. http://www.nytimes .com/2011/12/19/world/asia/air-force-drone-operators-show-high-levels-of -stress.html?_r=1.

Cixous, Hélène. *Tambours Sur La Digue, sous forme de piece ancienne pour marionettes jouee par des acteurs.* Paris: Theatre du Soleil, 1999.

Cloud, David S. "Transcripts of U. S. drone attack." *Los Angeles Times,* April 8, 2011.

———. "Anatomy of an Afghan war tragedy." *Los Angeles Times,* April 10, 2011.

Debord, Guy. *The Society of the Spectacle.* Exeter: Rebel Press AIM Publications, 1987.

Dickson, Andrew. "Ariane Mnouchkine and the Théâtre du Soleil: a life in theatre." *The Guardian,* Friday, August 10, 2012.

Di, Xin. "Lu Ban: The Great Master of Architecture and Trade Crafts." *Pure Insight.* Last modified November 10, 2008. http://www.pureinsight.org /node/5577.

Fanny and Alexander. DVD. Directed by Ingmar Bergman. New York: The Criterion Collection, 2011.

Favret, Mary A. *War at a Distance: Romanticism and the Making of Modern Wartime.* Princeton, NJ: Princeton University Press, 2010.

Glissant, Édouard. *Poetics of Relation.* Translated by Betsy Wing. Ann Arbor: The University of Michigan Press, 1997.

Graham, Stephen. *Cities Under Siege: The New Military Urbanism.* London: Verso, 2010.

Hardt, Michael and Antonio Negri. *Multitude: War and Democracy in the Age of Empire.* London: Hamish Hamilton, 2005.

Hell, Julia. "Remnants of Totalitarianism: Hannah Arendt, Heiner Müller, Slavoj Žižek, and the Re-Invention of Politics." *Telos* 136 (2006): 76–103.

Jenkins, Ron. "Theater: As if They Are Puppets at the Mercy of Tragic Fate." *The New York Times,* May 27, 2001.

Karzai, Hamid. "Karzai: Are You An American Puppet?" Interview by Becky Anderson. *CNN.* https://www.youtube.com/watch?v=riH-dNW9mY8.

Kellner, Douglas. "Ernst Bloch, Utopia, and Ideology Critique." In *Not Yet: Reconsidering Ernst Bloch,* edited by Jamie Owen Daniel and Tom Moylan. London: Verso, 1997.

Khan, Karim. "Transcript of the meeting with Karim Khan." Interview by Judy Bello and transcribed by Leah Bolger. *Fellowship of Reconciliation USA Archives* (November 25, 2012). http://archives.forusa.org/blogs/judy-bello /transcript-meeting-karim-khan/11398.

King, Martin Luther, Jr. "'Beyond Vietnam,' Address Delivered to the Clergy and Laymen Concerned about Vietnam, at Riverside Church. 4 April 1967." kingencyclopedia.stanford.edu. Accessed 5/21/2017.

Kliest, Heinrich von. "On the Marionette Theatre." In *On Dolls,* edited by Kenneth Gross and translated by Idris Parry. London: Notting Hill Editions, 2012. Kindle edition.

Kosek, Jake. "Ecologies of Empire: On the New Uses of the Honeybee." *Cultural Anthropology* 25, no. 4 (2010): 650–78.

Lal, Amit. "Micro and Nano Electro-Mechanical Systems: Technology Engineering Metamorphosis." Presentation at the DARPA's 25th Systems and Technology Symposium, Anaheim, CA, August 7, 2007. http://archive .darpa.mil/DARPATech2007/proceedings/dt07-mto-lal-micronano.pdf.

Lawton, Kim. "The Ethics of Drones." *Religion & Ethics Newsweekly* video, 8:49. August 26, 2011. http://www.pbs.org/wnet/religionandethics/2012/03/02 /august-26-2011-the-ethics-of-drones/9350/.

Löwy, Michael. *Fire Alarm: Reading Walter Benjamin's "On the Concept of History."* Translated by Chris Turner. London and New York: Verso, 2006.

Lukács, Georg. *History and Class Consciousness: Studies in Marxist Dialectics.* Cambridge, MA: The MIT Press, 1971.

Mills, Winifred H. and Louise M. Dunn. *Marionettes, Masks, and Shadows.* Garden City, New York: Doubleday, Doran & Company, 1931.

Mitchell, Robert. "Suspended Animation, Slow Time, and the Poetics of the Trance." *PMLA* 126, no. 1 (January 2011): 107–22.

Montaigne, Michel de. *The Complete Essays of Montaigne.* Translated by Donald M. Frame. Stanford, CA: Stanford University Press, 1958.

———. *Michel de Montaigne: The Complete Essays.* Translated by M. A. Screech. Harmondsworth, UK: Penguin. 1991.

Plato. *The Laws.* Translated by Trevor J. Saunders. New York: Penguin. 1970.

Rancière, Jacques. *The Emancipated Spectator.* London: Verso, 2009.

Rivera, Alex. "Border Control." Interview by Malcom Harris. *The New Inquiry* (July 2, 2012). https://thenewinquiry.com/features/border-control/.

Rockwell, John. "Theater; Behind the Masks of a Moralist." *The New York Times,* September 27, 1992.

Rousseau, Jean-Jacques. *Reveries of the Solitary Walker.* London: Penguin Classics, 1980.

Shaw, George Bernard. "Note on Puppets." In *Dolls and Puppets,* by Max Von Bochn and translated by Josephine Nicoll. New York: New York Cooper Square Publishers, 1966.

Solaris. DVD. Directed by Andrei Tarkovsky. New York: The Criterion Collection, 2002.

Sorgenfrei, Carol Fisher. "Production Review: *Tambours Sur Le Digue.*" *Asian Theatre Journal* 19, no. 1 (Spring 2002): 255–57.

Sparrow, Robert. "Building a Better WarBot: Ethical Issues in the Design of Unmanned Systems for Military Applications." *Science and Engineering Ethics* 15 (2009): 169–87.

Stewart-Steinberg, Suzanne. *The Pinocchio Effect: On Making Italians, 1860–1920.* Chicago: University of Chicago Press, 2007.

Sussman, Mark. "Performing the intelligent machine: deception and enchantment in the life of the automation chess player." In *Puppets, Masks, and Performing Objects,* edited by John Bell. Cambridge, MA: The MIT Press, 2001.

Virilio, Paul. *Pure War: Twenty-five Years Later.* Translated by Mark Polizzotti and Brian O'Keeffe. Los Angeles: Semiotext(e), 2008.

Wood, Paul. *Modernism in Dispute: Art Since the Forties.* New Haven: Yale University Press, 1993.

21ST CENTURY ESSAYS

David Lazar and Patrick Madden, Series Editors

A new series from The Ohio State University Press, 21st Century Essays is a vehicle to discover, publish, and promote some of the most daring, ingenious, and artistic new nonfiction. This is the first and only major series that announces its focus on the essay—a genre whose plasticity, timelessness, popularity, and centrality to nonfiction writing make it especially important in the field of non-fiction literature. In addition to publishing the most interesting and innovative books of essays by American writers, the series will publish extraordinary international essayists and reprint works by neglected or forgotten essayists, voices that deserve to be heard, revived, and reprised. The series is a major addition to the possibilities of contemporary literary nonfiction, focusing on that central, frequently chimerical, and invariably supple form: The Essay.

You, Me, and the Violence
Catherine Taylor

Curiouser and Curiouser: Essays
Nicholas Delbanco

Don't Come Back
Lina María Ferreira Cabeza-Vanegas

A Mother's Tale
Phillip Lopate